To Do List Formula

How to Increase Your Productivity and Master Your Time

William Richards

contained within this document, including, but not limited to, errors, omissions, or inaccuracies.

Table of Contents

Introduction

A day has 1,440 minutes – are you doing enough to make every minute count?

As humans, we are born procrastinators. The word tomorrow seems like our favorite word as we casually give in to the countless temptations that surround us. But how many hours or minutes are we actually spending doing things that take us closer to our long term goals? Are we doing enough to make them a reality or just giving in to how things are moving and at what pace?

Whenever we get down to listing the things we need to do to get "there", there is always tons on our to-do list. Take a moment to think about something you have been meaning to do in the past few days but haven't gotten around to doing. You know it will happen if you just squeeze in some time for it in the day. But isn't more time the one thing you keep running after and searching for? Even when you have all the necessary resources and action plans, you still fail to do it. Ever wondered why? What if the culprit is more than just your lazy bum? What if you really don't have the time or energy for it?

Here's the thing: the way you schedule tasks and goals and the way they are accomplished or delegated plays a crucial role. In a way, you can say it is directly proportional to your success or failure. How you use the limited amount of hours to your best means determines if you will come out as a victor or once again postpone it to a later date.

So, what matters is the way you manage your time and make the most of it. This is what this book is going to be about – time management.

Managing your time empowers you to achieve a greater control of your tasks and goals. When you can manipulate time on your terms, you feel more confident. You become better at dealing with the slip-ups that happen and respond accordingly, rather than just being blocked by them.

But before we talk more about time and the many different aspects of it, it is important that we discover what it truly means and more importantly, what it doesn't.

What Time Management Is and Isn't

Time management, in the simplest of terms, means planning and organizing multiple things in a given amount of time. It involves working smarter and not harder. It means getting more done in less time and adhering to deadlines and acing them. It is about not feeling the pressure of last-minute changes in routines because everything is sorted out in advance. It is about being efficient rather than just effective. Carla Crutsinger in her book *Thinking Smarter: Skills for Academic Success* defines time management as a process involving these components:

1. Goal setting

2. Task prioritization

3. Time allocation for each task

4. Adjustments in plans

5. Revisiting of priorities and goals periodically

6. Seeking results

Now that we understand what it is, we need to know what it isn't but often gets misunderstood.

Time management isn't about multitasking. It doesn't equate to doing multiple things at the same time. Doing more work, yes. Doing too many things, no. You have to understand the difference between the two to master time. We often see multitasking being labeled as a goal we all should aspire to, but recent studies prove how untrue that is. If anything, multitasking abstains from giving our 100% to each task and makes us switch between each back and forth. It is also reported to increase the overall time taken for each task completion which seems counterintuitive in nature. You just keep getting pulled from all directions and get sucked into the idea of doing more but not actually doing it. So what is time management then, you might wonder? It is about adhering to doing one task at a time, giving it the amount of attention and dedication it needs and being able to do it in less time and more efficiently. The brain doesn't have to fight between several ideas at once and can be better at problem-solving and rational thinking. This ultimately leads to getting tasks done in less time and of course, with more commitment.

Time management also doesn't mean that we need to stay busy all day and have a packed schedule. True, it does involve getting more done in less time but that doesn't translate to overlooking other important things in life. It is about making time for everything that holds value and importance and not just immersing yourself into crowded timetables.

It is about doing the things that result in the most profitability – both tangible and intangible. It is about prioritizing the most important tasks, ticking them off the list and later, taking out some quality time for interpersonal relationships. You can never taste success in life if it comes at the expense of relationships or poor health. You have to find that line where you need to stop and tell yourself that you need to take a break. In short, it isn't about tirelessly working yourself with no knowledge of the return on your investment. Think about it: what is the point of giving your all to a task that rarely gets you the returns you expected? It is like a sales manager replying to emails from angry customers rather than actually going out and locking some new ones in. Managing time involves whittling out all those tasks that aren't important. It is about identifying the ones that are worth giving a try, can be eliminated, outsourced or delegated.

Thirdly, another misconception regarding time management is that we think of it as something too robotic. We think of it as a strategy that is impossible to implement. We have this crazy idea of it meaning achieving perfectionism when all it tries to do is help you organize and schedule things better. No, you don't have to work every minute or second of the day. You don't have to feel drained of energy or find your mind too clouded and saturated to think anything else for the day. It shouldn't be something that stresses you out. On the contrary, it is something that reduces stress. We have to understand that it is very natural to lose the energy, motivation, drive and willpower that we started something with. Eventually, we are going to wear out. As the day progresses, we lose the drive and focus we hoped we would have when we initiated. With all the distractions around us, it is hard to maintain that level of oomph and excitement. The minute you find yourself staring off into space for no reason, you tell yourself that the approach is too robotic for anyone to follow through. It isn't supposed to be and if you feel like that, then maybe you don't know how to manage your time, after all.

Time management also doesn't mean giving your undivided attention to just one thing. A little contrary to what we discussed earlier, but hear this out. We have an attention span of eight seconds, which means we are designed to feel distracted after eight seconds. This is how just it is. How many times have you looked up from reading and not given something else your attention?

See we caught you, didn't we? Well, lucky for you, time management isn't about undivided focus. It doesn't mean that you have to engross yourself into hours and hours of uninterrupted work and maintain a steady focus. It involves taking small breaks to give your brain some time to refresh and restart. Ever noticed that sometimes we keep going back to the one idea we discarded earlier? Ever noticed how we keep tracing back to that more often as more time passes by? It is because the brain reaches a point of saturation and is unable to function in its full capacity when it lacks some relaxation time. If that is true, how should you go about each task? Well, here's the trick: time management allows for breaking each task into smaller chunks and viewing each chunk as a separate task itself. This means that you are doing the same amount of work but working on just one idea within an idea at a time and being done with it. The sense of accomplishment that follows and the little break times in between keep you motivated and your attention focused. Time management is about breaking tasks into smaller, more manageable ones and then getting them out of the way one at a time.

Next, many of us also assume that time management has something to do with the finish line. Here's a fun fact: you will never be able to get things done the way you expect to. We are all adults here. There is no reason to leave you with any false hope because there is no magical finish line that you will be able to reach with time management. Why are we being this harsh? It is because our resources are scarce. We are bound to stumble upon some uncertain or unseen circumstances. Avoiding these isn't what time management is about. It is about ensuring that you have all your top priority goals on, you guessed it – top! It involves making tough choices about what things cut and which ones not to. It is about investing logically after thorough evaluation. It is about working towards important outcomes. No one ever measures productivity with what's left undone. It is measured by what has been achieved and whether it is most profitable or not. An employee that works overtime but does poor work never gets promoted. It is always the dude Jim with the highest productivity. So when you seek to manage your time better, aim for the quality of the tasks accomplished rather than the amount of them.

And, finally, time management doesn't mean that you have to poke your nose at everything and be everywhere. It is more about scheduling what's important and what isn't. We often think that if we attend this year's biggest business event, we will put our brand in the limelight. However, it takes more than just word-of-mouth marketing to stand out. Your work has to stand out and to do that, you have to learn what things will get you heard and which won't. At the end of the day, it is all about what you choose to prioritize.

So let's get on with the book and see what more it has to offer in terms of tips and tricks. The overall goal of it is to help you identify the pitfalls that prevent you from finding your way to success and how being able to manage your time can make it a reality.

Chapter 1:

What is Time Management?

What is time? If we were to go back and learn about the concept of time and how we ever came to measure it with clocks and watches, it would take more than just one volume. But since it is important to have a greater understanding of what we are getting ourselves into, we shall try to make it as exciting and short as possible to keep you from slipping away.

There have been many ambiguities and contradictions when we talk about the concept of time. Some describe it as nothing more than an occurrence of events in a given sequence. Like the chicken coming in before the egg or the egg coming in before. It is about a laid pattern that everything in the universe follows. Some think of it as a resourceful element, which if lost or misplaced, is gone forever. Some see it as an approach to finishing a specific task by skillfully allotting it a set time beforehand whereas others divide it into two different categories – qualitative and quantities. When talking of qualitative time, they mean the time spent doing an activity and when talking about quantities aspect of it, they mean how it is measured in seconds, minutes, hours, days and weeks, etc.

When talking about the imperative role it plays in our lives and work, many think that it involves taking charge, developing a purpose, consciously setting priorities and carefully organizing. It is about engaging in difficulties, not merely shrinking underneath them. It is also seen as not the end but rather the means to an end. It is more about manipulating the course of events that take place rather than manipulating time itself.

Lastly, one can't emphasize more on the idea that it needs to be mastered by everyone no matter what their age, profession or employment type.

A Brief History of Time Management, a.k.a Efficiency

Ever wondered when did we ever come to terms with the need for efficiency in our lives? What led to us thinking that we lacked it and whoever came up with the idea to improvise and prioritize? Well, we have the answer. Someone (whose name we don't know) invented efficiency some 6000 years ago in the form of cuneiform writing. It was called upon by the Mesopotamians living on the banks of the Tigris and Euphrates rivers. They demanded a better record-keeping system and thus, it was the first time tracking done in writing.

Jumping to a few hundred years from them, we finally had the first attempts at time tracking during 3500 B.C. It was the Egyptians then who built tall pillars to keep track of time using shadows cast by the sun. This allowed them to divide the day in two halves. Later, they improved their original design by creating rudimentary sundials.

Those ancient civilizations also had their pay systems for employees. There was specific pay for specific work. The wages were determined by the amount of work done during the day —something we still use today!

Skipping a few centuries from then and entering the 18th century, we saw an increasing need for time management. This was when workers were upgraded to employees and got permanent places in offices and factories. One of the leading advocates for better time management systems in force was Benjamin Franklin. He was devoted to setting efficiency as a benchmark for professional and personal goals. He was also the first one to have ever uttered the phrase "Time is money." This led to many employers rethinking their wage policies and many came to the conclusion that the employees must only be paid for the hours they worked. Employees, conversely, were determined to ensure that they were being paid for the time they worked to the dot. Therefore, both the employers and employees allowed the system to remain transparent as well as become a preferred choice for both. This made tracking methods more accurate and also helped them emerge.

During that time, pen and paper were considered the primary way to keep track of time and money. However, sooner than later, employers realize that the system was quite time-consuming. It even involved some risk of bribery and false reporting as not every record seemed accurate. Therefore, bookkeeping errors became a norm until Willard Bundy stepped in, in 1888. Along with some other scientists and inventors, he developed several mechanical time-tracking devices to help businesses keep track of the hours worked. Today, many even call his clock-like time tracking devices Bundy clocks.

Later in the 19th century, we finally had Fred Flintstone show up to the scene and present his method of tracking time.

In the same century, Frederick Winslow published a book titled *The Principles of Management* that devised a management theory for factory managers. It entailed details of a management system that they could use to apply the best ways to do a job and cut out excess time. With guidelines about training and resources, the goal was to improve performance overall and apply the most time-effective methods to do any job.

Following that, leaders like Peter Drucker came forward with their theories that offered more inclusive ideas and also applied to white collar employees. His basic premise was to establish a system that catered to the need to manage enterprises by offering them an array of goals and wants rather than just subordinating an enterprise to a single value.

As we entered the 20th century, entire companies were built on finding the best time tracking solutions and improvise on Bundy's ideas for time clocks. This was the first time when time clocks were presented for the mass public and service-based industries. Access to computer technology was also introduced and many companies gave up on the idea of manually keeping employee time records and switched to digital. Not only did that involve less paperwork, there was also little chance to manipulate the evidence and record. Then we all went from using Excel to more advanced and accurate time tracking and managing systems.

Today, we have even surpassed that stage and all one needs to clock their time in and out is by swiping a card or punching in an identification number. All the records are stored digitally and can be accessed at all times.

So, you notice how man was always intrigued with the idea of managing time or making the most of it? Notice how he wouldn't stop at anything and continued to improvise and eliminate laborious tasks all the time? This is one reason why we need to keep using time management as well. So that tomorrow, we can be better at doing the things we do today. It is a constant struggle and one has to keep pace with it, too.

Why Precise Timing is Everything

But why is it so important to get the timing right for everything? Well, Daniel Pink might have an answer. In his book *When: The Scientific Secrets of Perfect Timing*, he proposes that not only is performing a task essential, how we do it is also important. When we fail to make the most of our time and not pay heed to how our actions may affect the consequences of our results, we end up with bad decisions. When we don't know how to manage time like it should be managed, it hinders our creativity. Think about it: do you really trust yourself to come up with the most creative ideas the night before a big presentation? Your goal isn't to aim for perfection then, but to just get it done with. This results in a poor-looking presentation, failing to impress everyone – even you. Now, imagine you had taken out the time to work on it for an hour every day of the week. Would you have still come up with the same presentation? No, it would have looked a hundred times better!

But how can one do that? Well, Pink offers insights for that too. He suggests that instead of viewing every project as linear, we should focus on not just the beginning of it, but also the middle and the end. You have to start with true passion, which most people usually do. However, it is the middle where they begin to slump. We often start a new job with great passion but as the first month or the next rolls in, we lose passion for what we do. This is where the problem truly begins. We start procrastinating and giving less than 100%. When we do that, it results in a poor ending because we have basically messed up in the middle. Even if we give our 100% then, we still will have to make up for the time we wasted in the middle. We have to account for it, too. Therefore, Pink believes that each section of any task, be it big or small, should be managed with care and attention. Each stage should be given the adequate time it requires.

Having said that, we have to emphasize on the benefits time management offers in both our work and personal lives. Only then will we be able to convince ourselves that we really need it in our lives. The benefits of time management are as follow:

At Work

How many of us love what we do? Or believe that we can have all our goal sets for the day accomplished before the end of it? Or are able to make the most of our time? Even the greatest world leaders and entrepreneurs haven't gotten to the point where they can make that remark. Take Elon Musk, for example. The guy works countless hours, barely has time to sleep and yet wishes that there were more hours in the day so that he could manage both accordingly (Umoh, 2018). However, if we are deliberately wasting the amount of time allotted to us during work hours and not working at our best, then what is the point anyways? Is the biggest part of your life only about getting a check at the end of every month? It has got to be more than that. Moreover, nearly all of us, at some point, have complained about the lack of time on our hands. Due to work commitments we have missed out on birthday parties, or other important events because we have to get something done.

If only you knew of the benefits of time management and knew how to do it, you would know that you can get out of making such excuses and missing important events with your families and friends forever. Let's explore a few below.

Reduces Stress Levels

Even the most competent of executives and employees feel the pressure of keeping up with important deadlines and ensuring that everything gets done in the best manner possible. After all, it is all about their reputation!

We all lead busy lives and have trouble maintaining work-life balance which leads to an unstable and unhappy life. This induces stress in our systems. However if, hypothetically, we began completing everything on time or better, before the deadline, just imagine the relief and comfort! This is one of the biggest perks of time management. It leaves us with ample amount of time to enjoy both our work and social life and eliminate stress altogether. When one isn't stressed, they are better at doing things. The quality of work improves drastically as well.

Enhances Productivity

Continuing from the point above, improved productivity is another benefit. Ever had one of those days where nothing seemed to go as planned? There are mistakes in the report, missing data on the presentation, problems with the PC, a file gone missing, etc. All of these things can have a drastic impact on your overall productivity. Even when given the extra time to work on those issues, we somehow fail to make significant progress. Ineffective productivity is like cutting a lemon with a blunt knife. It isn't going to happen and when it does, it isn't going to look pretty. Another important factor that affects our productivity negatively is lack of breaks in between. Good time management ethics allows individuals to enjoy time intervals mid-work. They are pre-planned and help the mind get some rest and reduce the chances of fatigue and tiredness. A good practice of time management encompasses knowing when to stop, when to work and when to rest.

Reduced Thoughts about Procrastination

Any work that doesn't involve our liking often gets pushed to the last minute. Even the most successful of us have procrastinated and put off things to a later date. However, when we learn the importance of time and how valuable it is, the idea of procrastination rarely messes with our head. We prefer doing things at the allotted time rather than delaying it.

Less Wasted Time

When you have everything planned out in advance, organized and good to go, there are fewer chances of any time getting wasted. When everyone knows what is expected of them and when, time is spent wisely. The time saved can be invested in other important things or spent with family and friends.

Good Habits Take Over

Like self-discipline, empathy and mental focus, time management is also a skill which, if it becomes a habit, allows the individual to become a better human being. When we become punctual and organize better, we set an example for others to follow, too. When we practice positive habits like time management in our daily life, our chances of growing responsibly also improve.

More Self-Confident

When one feels in control of their life and all the choices in it, confidence comes from within. You remain in the authoritative position and feel mentally strong. You can make the most of your time and prioritize the things that need prioritizing. Also, when you feel more in control, you are likely to work harder and focus better. With time management and self-discipline, there is no stopping you.

Increased Chances of Advancements

Ever wondered why people who worry so much about doing the right thing at the right time are so successful at everything they do? It is because they know what Ben Franklin meant when he said time is money. They understand how valuing time for what it is, is the way to get to the top. Successful world leaders develop habits like time management, which have a trickle-down effect. When they apply time management strategies to minimize the amount of time required to accomplish a certain task, it leaves them with more free time to spend on things that will take them to the top. It can be anything like learning a new skill, enrolling in a more advanced class, taking up a new hobby, or giving their dreams some direction. Your chances to get a better job, promotion, or just more recognition due to your new skill increase and so do the opportunities to grow further.

On the other hand, people who never get anything done on time are rarely the ones being promoted. They also happen to be the ones who are always complaining about unfair biases. Here's the thing: if you aren't going to put in the effort and still expect to be showered with opportunities, you are never going to make it, be it in your career or personal life. You have to take the reins in your hands and do the work it needs. Make time for things that will help you succeed in your career and personal life.

In Relationships

Relationships require effort. They need love, communication and trust to stay bound. But not many people realize that they also need quality time. Your family shouldn't have to suffer because of your poor time management habits. They shouldn't have to put up with excuses in your place because you are busy elsewhere. They shouldn't have to suffer because you can't make it to your own surprise birthday party. They shouldn't have to deal with your shortcomings and your bad temper over how they are always falling short on time.

You have to make time and find that work-life balance. Your family and friends should always come first before your work and the best way to make that happen is getting done with everything on time at the office so that when you come home to your family, you are there with them. Learning to manage time will surely make you the best partner, parent or friend. Here are some of the ways time management will drastically improve your relationships and you will finally free yourself from fights that result due to lack of quality time.

It Improves Communication

One of the biggest reasons for fights among couples is the lack of communication which can be partly blamed on the lack of time between the partners. Does your partner feel that you are never there for them? Do they feel that you are neglecting the kids? Do they complain of living in the room like two roommates and not partners? If so, then maybe you need to make time to sit down and communicate things better. This is only possible when you actually take out the time, perhaps on the weekend or every other night to have a conversation with your partner. All they want from you is to ask them how their day was or how the kids were doing in school. They might need some help with the chores or just want to talk to someone to feel heard. Good time management ethic will help you stay connected with your family and allow you to lead a happier life.

It Rekindles the Passion

Sometimes, the spark of love fades away. It is one of the most common issues marriage counsellors deal with daily. Couples come in complaining about how they don't feel connected to one another anymore and one of the biggest reasons is the lack of time. They are told things like, "Go on a short vacation," or, "Go on dinner dates like old times." It comes down to spending quality time together, once again. You notice how everything has to do with how we manage time? Remember the good old days when our fathers would come home from work and then take us out for ice cream or to playland? How did they ever manage to do that? These are some of the fondest memories we have with them. It's because when they came back from work, they made sure they left work at the office. They didn't spend time making calls over the dinner table or replying to emails while playing with their kids. They were wholly invested and that is what made them different from the parents of today.

We are so consumed by the Internet and technology that we have begun taking each other for granted. We have devalued the need for human emotion and feelings and this is why we see such a spiking divorce rate everywhere in the world.

With proper time management, we can rekindle the lost spark and make time for our partners. We can take out the time to do things you two enjoy doing and stay interested in each other. That way, the spark will stay ignited forever.

It Fosters the Sense of Togetherness

When you manage time accordingly and spend it working on your relationship, you let the other person know that they are valued. This makes them value you in return. Such relationships where time spent together is a priority are more likely to last longer because partners are close to each other, share things together, have open communication, value individual interests and work to keep the relationship healthy and stable. But all of this is only possible when time is managed and relationships are prioritized.

It Allows You to De-stress

Sometimes, relationships can become stressful, especially when one partner feels like they arc doing all the work to keep the relationship stable. The other partner is usually out of the picture, leaving the first partner to handle everything from grocery shopping to paying the bills to dealing with the kids. This can become extremely stressful and the lack of help from the other spouse just adds to that pressure. This isn't acceptable behavior since the partner making all the effort starts to feel neglected, unappreciated and burdened. Now, imagine the other partner putting in equal work, helping with the chores, driving around the kids, buying the groceries and spending time with the family. This will leave the first partner with time of their own and allow them to de-stress. They will no longer feel burdened or feel like the pressure of doing everything right is on them alone. Therefore, you need to make the time instead of being absent from a relationship you vowed to be a part of.

Lack of Discipline Gets You Nowhere

Now that we have established the importance and benefits of time management, we can't leave without discussing the detriments of what will happen if one doesn't manage time. This leads us to the discussion about what happens to those who waste it. More importantly, we need to understand why we waste time. Is it because we are afraid that we will fail eventually and thus postpone things until the last minute? Is fear stopping us from giving our 100%? One of the reasons we fear failure is that we think that we will not be able to recover if we fail. Others fear being judged by others over their choices. As humans, we have this odd habit of pulling each other's leg. We want to bring everyone down by mocking them, criticizing their way of doing things, and laughing at them. Shouting out opinions to deliberately bruise someone's ego and feelings is one reason why so many people fear change. Even when they know that what they are doing will ultimately help them succeed in life, they still don't try. They fear what others will think or say about them.

Firstly, we need to understand that fear is important in life, too. If it stops us from trying new things, it also keeps us from going forward with the bad and negative ones. Therefore, some form of fear is essential. Moreover, it is also the one thing, which if we overcome, leaves us feeling satisfied and like a winner. Ever had that feeling of happiness and victory gush over you when you overcame something you never thought you would? The reward seems so much bigger and better, doesn't it?

Secondly, there are times when fate will be on your side and you will achieve things easily. It would feel like they just keep coming to you and thus you feel that you don't need to change anything and let things flow as they are flowing. This is another reason why so many people don't value the importance of time management. It is because they have gotten things effortlessly. They are privileged to afford being late and still get away with the best as opposed to someone who spends their whole life trying to make things better but fails miserably.

Keeping these factors aside, what you need here is a self-assessment of whether you are making the most of your time or not. Knowing so will further facilitate you in identifying any such opportunities that you had been missing out on due to lack of time management. For instance, you might realize that you spend almost 3 to 4 hours per day engrossed in your phone, browsing social media.

Are You a Time Waster?

Remember how, when we were young, we would talk about what we wanted to be when we grew up? Some of us wanted to be astronauts, some of us wanted to be doctors, engineers, or athletes. How many of us actually became what we dreamt of? Not many, I reckon or else you wouldn't be reading this book in the first place. Ever wondered why we never got to fulfilling our dreams despite having the best education, supportive parents, and bright prospects and grades? One of the biggest reasons we failed to be what we wanted to be is because we didn't value time or make the most of it when we had the chance. We still had to study to get where we are today, so why didn't we study for what we wanted to be? Those who didn't have their dreams fulfilled often have the same thing in common: they wasted their time. Let's hope you don't find yourself in the same situation.

You Do Everything on Your Own

There are some things that you have to delegate or set a specific time for. Not everything is your responsibility. This is what most budding entrepreneurs and businessmen don't understand. It is one thing to keep a check and balance of all the processes and run out to get everything done on your own, and another if you have burdened yourself with more than you can handle. There is a chance that you are putting off important things in favor of unimportant ones. Think about it; if you are the owner of your company, it isn't your job to attend to every customer and client call, respond to emails, run after the suppliers and be on the site all the time to check everything goes smoothly. Instead, focus on things that are more likely to help you build a bright future and name for your business. Spend time figuring out what more can you do to streamline your processes better, invest time in looking at what your competitors are doing, spend time reaching out to newer clients and study the latest market trends to stay ahead of your game.

If you are not doing any of that, then yes, you are a time waster.

You Complain Too Much

You do more talk and less work. Your actions don't match your words. You are all about making plans and daydreaming but when it comes to actually getting down to doing the work, you don't follow through. Moreover, when things don't turn out the way you wanted them to, you complain and feel dissatisfied. You nag but aren't ready to work. You complain about being treated unfairly at work, you aren't content with your pay scale, and you are always whining about your boss or superiors. If this sounds like the person you see in the mirror every day, then it's time to change.

You Rarely Think

On the other hand, you make hasty decisions all the time which means that not all of them will be sensible and profitable. This, again, happens because you choose to waste your time over meaningless and unimportant things or have the habit of procrastinating until the very last minute which leaves you with no time to think things through and just go with whatever is available. Imagine you are the head chef of a renowned restaurant that has gotten poor reviews recently. Despite being told a month before that food inspectors will be visiting any time, you still don't make any changes to the menu or work on the hygiene and cleanliness factor of your kitchen. Then one day, the food inspectors pay a surprise visit and you find yourself in trouble with disorganization and unhygienic work conditions. So you hide all the things you can behind the freezer or in it, hoping the inspectors won't spot them. What are your chances of surviving that surprise visit? Few, right?

Spend time thinking and evaluating what will be best for your business and family all the time. Don't put off important decisions for the eleventh hour; be proactive and wise with your choices.

You Underestimate Yourself

Another factor that makes you a member of the time waster's list is that you think very little of yourself. You think you don't have it in you to change your circumstances so you accept how they are. You are too critical of your choices and often doubt your capabilities. You also find yourself comparing yourself with others, and thus feel even more unqualified. Self-questioning is important in life but it can also be something that ruins you. How so? It is because it stops you from trying new things or improvising existing ones.

You Don't Have Concrete Plans

It is all good and well to stay in the present and focus on the now. But that doesn't mean you don't have to have a plan for the future. Having something to look forward to serves as the motivation you need to stick it out when dealing with roadblocks and bumps during your journey. Having an end goal is what allows you to keep moving forward and make the best use of the available resources, including time. If you don't have something to look forward to, chances are you will waste time. If you are someone without a plan, you are like a wandering boat in the ocean with no destination to go to. You can't let that happen.

You must have a detailed plan with laid out instructions and steps to get there so that you stay focused and motivated and don't waste time over pointless things.

You Spend Time with the Wrong Lot

Are you someone who hangs around losers? This isn't meant to be insulting, but certain people in life haven't achieved much and thus aren't the best kind of gang to hang around with. They don't offer any valid advice that will help you prosper. If they had it, they would have used it themselves. Spending too much of your precious time with them is like wasting it. You need to be around people who lift your spirit and drive you. Just knowing about their struggles and how they overcame them is in itself a great inspiration to have. You should aspire for that, too. Time spent with them isn't wasted as you always come out feeling more empowered and motivated to work past your struggles.

Therefore, be with people who help you improve. Spend time with those who don't believe or support stagnation in life and are always striving to be better. If you spend time with people who have nothing good to offer but only talk about how miserable their life is, they will drain every ounce of energy from your system until you become one of them and stop trying.

Your Workplace is a Mess

Whether you freelance or work in a 50-story empire building, your work environment plays a crucial role in determining how much time you utilize or waste throughout the day. If you work from home and do freelance gigs at a designated desk, look at how organized/disorganized it looks. Is there an empty coffee mug, scraps of paper, cluttered stationery and chargers, etc.? Is your desktop screen filled with unorganized folders or perhaps you have uncountable tabs opened at once, many of which aren't even work-related?

If you work in an office, does it depict a similar picture with only more folders on the desk, plus sticky notes on the walls or the side of the desktop screen? Let me guess, you must have a hard time looking for things when they are needed. You must have to sort through drawers, injure your hand with the paper clips/stapler pins and have an overflowing dustbin. Did you know that disorganization is one of the most undervalued time wasters?

If you are someone who has to spend half of the time looking through their desk and drawers, then you are a time waster. You lack the basic work ethic which is aimed at making your life easier. Ever thought why were folders and stationary holders invented in the first place? They were invented so that you can stop spending so much time looking for your stationary or important documents. The sooner you find something you are looking for, the sooner you can move onto the next thing and save time.

You Take Too Many Breaks

You are a time waster if you rely religiously on breaks. The problem doesn't lie in taking the breaks, the problem lies when you don't get back to work after you are done with the break. Imagine this: you yawned for the fifth time and knew that it was time to brew a cup of coffee from the kitchen at work. You saved all the work on your desktop and got up to head towards the coffeemaker. Someone in the office had the same idea and you two meet in the kitchen and strike up a conversation about how the day is dragging so slow and how you wished it would just be the end of the day already. Small chit chat turns into a conversation that lasts until the hot coffee in your mug is cold. You two finally head back to your workstations only to realize that you have wasted half an hour of work. All the tasks that were in the pipeline are pushed forward and despite your best efforts, you still leave for home with some of them on the to-do list. Frequent and careless break times can be big time wasters because it gets hard to get back to work once we come back from them.

You Socialize Too Much

Following from the same point above, spending too much time surrounded by chatty co-workers can also lower your productivity and chances of success. If you have the habit of stopping at every co-worker's work station when you get up for some chore like Xeroxing, you are not only wasting your time but also theirs. Of course, fostering a healthy work environment is important as no one can spend the whole day in silence, but you have to limit the baseless talks when you have too much left to do. In case you aren't the one making all the noise, use headphones to drown out the noise coming from other workstations so that you don't break your levels of concentration with every bit of laughter and hi-five. Ensure that the time you have designated to work on something is utilized doing just that. You can socialize with your co-workers during lunch and after-work hours.

You Refuse to Seek Clarification

Many employees feel ashamed when they think they will have to seek help from their superiors or co-workers. They fear being judged over their lack of skills and thus, keep making blunders and wasting time. Getting some clarification over how to do it or how the client expects it to be done isn't harmful for your reputation, but making blunders is. Would you rather be degraded by putting something up that isn't correct or would you prefer asking someone for help so that you don't look like a fool? Think about it!

Stop telling yourself that you will eventually figure it out, especially when it isn't your area of expertise. You are only letting your pride get in the way which, by the way, won't get you very far. If you value time and not the opinions of others, there is a greater likelihood that you will be appreciated for seeking clarity and not wasting time by coming up with something wrong.

You Lack a Purpose

Without a clear-cut and well-directed purpose in life, there is little hope that you will learn to manage time. A purpose in life offers motivation. It makes one give their absolute best. It allows them to keep on moving. It helps them keep their focus sharp. It makes them forgive all the mistakes in the past. Having a long-term goal to look forward to is imperative. Without some bigger picture, you will fritter away your time which benefits no one. If you want to work on your productivity levels, establish a better focus, and stay motivated, you need a clear picture of where you want to see yourself a few years from now. Without an incentive for staying focused, it isn't hard to waste another day. You will easily give in to the temptation of whatever seems interesting, as there is nothing that keeps your mind committed. It takes severe determination and time management ethic to get somewhere in life. If you don't have that, then you will remain a time waster all your life.

Chapter 2:

Dealing With Time Wasters

In the first chapter, we concluded with whether a person is a time-waster or not. But what if a time-waster can be something other than a person, too? What if it is something that detracts, distracts, distances or diverts someone from the planned activities, goals, tasks and appointments? Therefore, to not leave the possibility hanging out in the air, we shall be elaborately discussing time wasters that aren't people but rather things and activities, environments, projects, tasks and even meetings, that make one become one. We are talking about activities that derail even the most carefully laid out plans and lead to either procrastination or poor productivity.

Firstly, we must know that time wasters are preventable in most cases. They are usually in one's control but can, at times, be external in nature – ones we have little control over. Although we can't do much about the external time-wasters such as an urgent call or meeting, or a family emergency that one has to attend to, we must try to prevent the ones that we can, whenever we can. That way, even when something unexpected does come up, we don't have to scrap everything from our calendars and start over. Some minor adjustments here and there should do the job, right? The good news is that as soon as we spot them we can reprioritize things and avoid wasting time on them.

So let's begin with listing down all the possible time wasters that are affecting your productivity and leading to poor overall performance, a.k.a reducing your chances of reaching success.

Emails

Email is usually one of the first things that one checks as they get started with their day. It is also one of the biggest time wasters. Did you know that more than 200 billion emails get sent and received per day across the globe? Did you also know that on average, an employee checks their email some 30+ times an hour? That makes it roughly about 240 times per day during a 9-5 shift (The Shocking Truth about How Many Emails are Sent, 2019). The pop-ups can be quite distracting. It is so easy to get away with the temptation to click on them and see what they contain the second they pop-up. Of course, urgent emails from clients and superiors are to be responded to promptly, but many times, the emails are just promotional in nature. They are from our social media accounts and deals, coupons, and newsletters from the websites we have subscribed to. The thing that makes them a time-waster is that once we open them, we are tempted to go to the website and browse the deals. This wastes time and the work that we were previously doing gets delayed. Sometimes, the break continues for up to an hour which is why one needs to limit the time spent on checking emails and set a time to reply to them after the tasks have been done.

Social Media Automation

Though it is one of the fastest mediums to stay updated about the lives of your family, friends and favorite celebrities, social media sites are also one of the biggest time wasters. On average, one spends about 136 minutes on social media per day as per the statistics presented by Statista in 2018 (Clement, 2018). That is almost two hours of wasted time. And that statistic takes into account usage by all demographics. If we just take into account the social media usage per day by teenagers and adults in their 30s and 40s, the ratio is likely to hit somewhere between 3 to 4 hours with ease. Unless you work as a social media manager, there is no need for you to spend so much time on it, especially when there is so much work to do. Social channels should be treated with care as they can affect one's productivity and concentration.

Poor or No Skills

We did shed some light over this earlier but it needs to be stressed upon once again. Lack of skills isn't a time waster, but wasting time attempting to do tasks without them is indeed one. You should always be willing to try new things but trying to take over things you have no knowledge of or expertise in is only going to take much longer. Picture this: your computer is hit by a virus. There are two options to deal with the problem. First, you can just pick up the phone and let the administration know so that they can send the computer technician to have a look at it and second, you try to fix it on your own. Although the first seems less time-consuming, many of us try to DIY solutions ourselves. You think that reading a few articles on Google will help you fix it so you get started on it on your own. If you valued your time, you would have never taken up the job and would have chosen the first option. Not to mention, a lack of knowledge is a dangerous thing. You might end up causing more harm and lose valuable data while trying to get the virus fixed.

If you are not an expert at something or have little knowledge of how to do it, it is better to seek help from someone who knows how to fix things.

Noisy Coworkers

Noisy coworkers don't offer a productive work environment. The constant chit-chatting is the kind of disturbance that keeps you distracted from your work or takes your mind off it from time to time. This makes your coworkers time wasters too as they aren't contributing anything beneficial to you. Amidst the pressure of getting things right and done with before the end of the day, you have to keep distractions to a minimum and maintain your focus. Sadly, a noisy work environment doesn't promise that!

TV and Movies

This is especially for all those working professionals who go home only to spend their remaining waking time slouching in front of a TV or binging a series on Netflix. This is no way to spend the day. Have you already not given your eyes a tiresome day at work by looking directly at the screen all day? Do you have to make them go through some more torture when you get home? Many of you might say that the reason you watch television is to give your mind some cool off time, but let me ask you this: in a world that survives on commercials and breaking news every next hour, with sports events rigged and betted on, is there anything worth watching? Sometimes, it feels more depressing than our high-pressure jobs.

If we take TV shows into account, just the decision to start something new and follow it until the season ends is tiresome on its own. It's awkward that the more choices we have, the harder it becomes to pick just one. So even if you are watching something, which is fine by all means, the time you waste in deciding what to watch is what serves as time wasted.

Using Tools Incompetently

Tools like online spreadsheets, website traffic metrics, planners, to-do list apps and, speech-to-text converters are all tools that are there for a reason. They are meant to reduce the time spent on things like excel sheets, manual logging, bookkeeping, important memos, task lists, etc. They are there to help you improvise and get things done faster and more effectively. However, if you are not advancing with them and still use the old methods to do things, then you're not helping yourself at all. You need to learn how to use them and later, use them to save time and invest it elsewhere. Automation of tasks also limits redundancies and chances of errors.

Not Saying No

How many of us have committed to things we didn't want to do just so we would not be thought of as nerds and workaholics? Sometimes, we commit because we don't want to disappoint others, which is fair as long as doing so has some perks. For instance, committing to go to an important industry event so that you can build some networks and connect with prospective clients is a win-win for you and your business. The same goes for attending events like marriages, birthday parties, and holiday festivities with friends and family.

However, saying yes to things that offer no considerable benefits accounts for wasting your time. When you do that, you do yourself a big disservice. If you don't have the time in your schedule, let the expectant know in a humble but stern manner so that you can't be further pushed into doing it. Many people like to take advantage of our need to say yes. If your boss is expecting you to write a book in his/her name without decreasing your workload, then that accounts as taking advantage. Apologize politely and promise to make time for it when you have some. That way, you don't say no or yes.

Massive To-do Lists

Let's get one thing clear first. To-do lists are life-savers. They are the mayo that holds the burger together. They are the glue that fixes things. They are the only things that lay in between task generation and task completion. They reduce the amount of stress one feels when overwhelmed with too much work. They also help one stay true to the work and maintain a steady focus. They hold all the steps needed to get each task done.

However, it should be understood that although it helps one plan things strategically, having a bulky to-do list can do the exact opposite. It can make one feel stressed out rather than relieved. It can leave one feeling the jitters as they don't know where to start from. It can make one feel demotivated and procrastinate instead of improving their productivity. Excess of anything is bad and this is true in this case, too. Therefore, start with short to-do lists. You can create a new one once you are done with the existing one. It shouldn't matter as long as everything on it gets ticked off in the allotted time. Just keep them short to not let the pressure get the best of you.

Unnecessary Gatherings

On average, some 25 million meetings happen every day in the U.S alone (Perlow, Eun, & Hadley, 2017). These include all first-timer appointments, interview calls, and big corporation events and galas. Many executives deem these meetings and gatherings as nothing but a waste of time, as rarely does something productive come out of them. Many even go to such lengths as calling them a waste of time and money, which, quite frankly, is true. When was the last time you went to a conference or workshop and came out feeling like everything in your life was going to change? Even when they are meant to be inspirational and productive, some meetings and gatherings never deliver what is promised and are nothing but a waste of time. Ideally, all meetings should end within an hour or two. This is only possible when the goals of the meeting have already been set earlier and everyone going in has a clear idea of what to expect out of it. Next, there should be a set time for it to happen and it shouldn't be dragged deliberately. They should also start on time with the motto that the overall goal should be to improve existing conditions and boost productivity. Lastly, they should only be about the most important things and not about things that can easily be discussed via a call or in an email.

Addiction to Smartphones

Smartphones – the technology which was aimed at making our lives easier has become a nuisance today. On one hand, they allow us to connect efficiently but on the other, are quite addictive in nature. If someone were to say that we use smartphones for everything but communicating today, it wouldn't be wrong. Did you know an average person spends three hours and fifteen minutes per day glued to their phones (Matei, 2019)? And this only applies to employees and working-class individuals. But we don't do it intentionally. It all comes down to how our brains are designed to feel and act. They are hardwired to get a pleasure hit by the chemical dopamine whenever the phone buzzes, vibrates or pings.

But one can't deny the fact that it can become a time-waster when other things get delayed because of it. If, by the end of the day, it is the one thing that causes many chores on your to-do list to push for another day, this is a sign it is a time-waster.

Commute

One of the most underrated time wasters is traveling. Whether you take the subway to work, your car or ride a bicycle, you lose a few good minutes to an hour every day getting to and from work. And that average only increases when you get stuck in rush hour. Now, if you were to estimate the amount of time lost during commuting per year, you will have lost one or more days of work. But since this can't be avoided and must be endured, you must learn to utilize that time efficiently. For instance, if you have to take the subway every day and that takes away some good 45 minutes of your morning, how about using that time to read through a report, check your emails, or go through any presentation slides you need to go through? The point is, whatever you do, make sure you are not wasting time.

Multitasking

Not long ago, multitasking was all the rage. People were jumping to fill in their to-do lists with more than they could handle, hoping they would be able to get more done if they multitasked. However, the opposite proved true. Multitasking took more time, sustained poor focus and hampered one's productivity and concentration. It was then that the scientists began to rethink the approach to doing things and discovered that single-tasking, which had always been the norm, was more beneficial. New research also suggests that our brain isn't designed to take on multiple things at once. It can only focus better when working on a single thing (Sanbonmatsu, Strayer, Medeiros-Ward, & Watson, 2013). Even when we try to do multiple things simultaneously, the brain doesn't think about them all at once. Instead, it goes back and forth with different ideas, more like switching between tasks.

Therefore, you can say that those who indulge in multitasking are wasting their time as the overall time to complete all those tasks increases and one also can't guarantee undivided focus and improved quality.

Aiming for Perfection

Finally, people who aim for perfection or have extremely high standards rarely stay devoted to things. They keep finding small mistakes and keep trying to improve already-perfect things. It is understandable that many times, we are tempted to keep going back and redoing things to refine them. But it isn't always necessary and we need to know when to stop. When we keep going back and forth revising things, we are doing nothing but wasting time. Being a perfectionist isn't always a blessing in disguise. It can throw you off when the revisions make no difference. Perfection is impossible to achieve and it only kills your productivity. Think about it: if given an assignment, would you still function at your best when asked to revise it for the fifth time? You will start to detest the very idea of revisions and prefer spending your time elsewhere. Therefore, always aim for quality and not perfection!

Dealing with Time Wasters

To learn to manage things that waste time, we first need to divide them into two distinct categories. As stated before, some time wasters are external. They aren't in our control. For instance, a flight delay is a time waster but it isn't in our control. The other category is self-generated or internal time wasters. These are man-created in nature such as procrastination, checking emails when work is pending or setting up unnecessary meetings. Self-generated time wasters are controllable with better prioritizing and planning. Let's see how these can be managed accordingly.

External Time-Wasters

Calls

Calls aren't always that important. Some can be sent straight to voicemail and responded to later so that the momentum of work doesn't break. The best way to handle calls is to set a time every day to get back to the callers. That way, you won't have to take them in between tasks and spend more time getting back to it later. Additionally, when taking calls, aim to come to the point straight away without meaningless chit chat. Short conversations where the most important stuff gets discussed are the best, especially in work environments because time wasted is lost money.

Emails

Emails are the sneakiest ones to handle. The back-to-back notifications on the corner of your screen are enough to cause distraction. Add to that the tempting titles and subtitles. You simply can't resist clicking on them and that is what leads to wastage of time. Sorting through each email and determining if it's worth replying to right away or can be scheduled for later is a tough task. There are many ways to handle emails such as designating a specific time after every few hours to go through the important ones, or creating separate folders for work-related and promotional emails or snoozing the notification for promotional or social media-related emails for a later time in the day, etc. The only goal should be to understand the need to manage them so that productivity can't be affected.

Visitors

Visitors include everyone from your colleagues, to clients, to superiors just wanting to have a chat, and friends and family members. They can eat up your time without you even realizing it. They need to be handled with care so that they don't feel ignored or disregarded. The best way to do so is by keeping the talk short and changing positions while doing it. For instance, if a coworker comes up to your station and starts to chit chat, pick up your cup from the desk and stand up, holding it. You won't have to say a thing as the coworker will sense that you plan to head to the coffee machine and cut short the conversation. This gives the impression that you are in a hurry and thus helps with keeping the interaction short. Another smart way to avoid interaction when you have your room, say in the house, or the office, is to position your desk in such a manner that your back faces towards the door. That makes you seem less approachable.

Self-Generated Time Wasters

Procrastination

Being one of the most common forms of time wasters, it is only fair that we start with this one. Procrastination can be dealt with in many ways, many of which shall be discussed in detail in the following chapter. However, if you are looking for a quick heads up, you can always start with setting deadlines and break times for every task at hand. You can also set rewards for yourself when the task is accomplished so that you stay motivated to get it done. You must also aim to get started with the most important thing first so that, even if you do fall prey to procrastination later in the day, you won't feel guilty about something important being left out. Finally, you can set timers for all tasks and switch onto the next one once the time is up. That way, you will be keener to perform the first task so that you don't have it lying around for later.

Lack of Priorities

Setting priorities and proper planning are requisite for all tasks. You must always have a plan of action before commencing. Not having one leads to disorganization and procrastination. Make sure that you are accompanied by a to-do list of all the tasks you need to finish at all times. Additionally, ensure that they all follow a pattern so that everything stays in order. If the list contains more than you can handle, create another list containing all those priority tasks that need to be dealt with right away. There are several methods to prioritizing tasks and you should use them.

Disorganization

Be it digital or physical, be it in your office, car or home, it can be extremely time-wasting. People who are disorganized waste precious time searching for things. A disorganized work station means you won't be getting your hands on your stationery when you need it, a disorganized drawer means you will have a hard time finding that one folder your boss requests immediately, and a disorganized home means you will be spending double the time putting things back in their place. Aim to have a clutter-free work station so that your focus isn't hampered. Have all the resources you will or might need before starting something so that you don't have to look for it in the middle of a task.

Create Work-Life Balance

This is for everyone and anyone who has trouble managing their time. Remember when our parents worked for 8 hours straight from morning to evening and came back home after that? They never complained about the stress of work, fatigue or even lack of productivity. They seemed fine and happy with their jobs. Then why is it that despite having flexible work hours, better leave policies and work from home facilities, we still complain about fatigue, poor concentration, and stress? It is because we have let our work get on our nerves. We have allowed it to come before our family and relationships. We have deemed it more important hoping that it will make us content. However, what we fail to realize is that no one ever achieved all by working long and hard. Remember the saying, all work, and no play makes Jack a dull boy? It is exactly like that. We have to allow our minds to relax and stop when saturation takes over. We have to give it some time to cool off and indulge in activities other than work, just like our parents did.

Learn to Delegate

There are many things that you must do. But there are also many that you shouldn't do. As an individual hoping to save some time and invest it elsewhere, you must learn to differentiate between the tasks that need you from the tasks that don't. You have to know what things are worth investing your time in and what aren't. You must learn to delegate so that you can have more time for things that matter.

Prioritize Better

Prioritizing is, again, pivotal. You must know what deserves the first, second, and third place. You must create a to-do list of tasks ranked on their level of priority. This way, you can avoid wasting time doing unimportant or urgent tasks and use your energy, mind, and commitment on something more profitable.

Eliminate Distractions

Aim to avoid distractions of all sorts. This includes noise, environment, technology and even people. You must learn to value the little time you have and make the most of it by eliminating distractions from the day. It is a given fact that as you head further into the day, you lose the momentum and zest you had when you started. And if distractions keep hampering your focus, chances are you will lose that momentum sooner than you think.

Why Do We Fail To Resist Temptation?

Since we are on the topic of losing momentum and what role distractions play in it, it is also important to understand why we give in to them so easily. Just a text from someone or a notification about a new friend request and we go into the spiral of opening one tab after another, going through mutual friends, browsing through the photos, looking at the tags, and whatnot. It feels so convenient, doesn't it? And the worst part, we don't even feel guilty about it. Therefore, we must understand why we have such little control over our urges and why we fail to resist such temptations.

It is believed that self-control and willpower have to do something about it. Although we all possess that innate sense of self-righteousness which allows us to differentiate between the right and the wrong, we still fall prey to the temptations and forget the thin line that is between them.

Enter the Marshmallow Test experiment.

Some 40 years ago, Walter Mischel, a psychologist and Ph.D, conducted an experiment on self-control in kids. Although it was supposed to be a simple experiment, it turned out to be one of the most thought-provoking experiments in the world. Even today, it is regarded as insightful and anyone learning psychology is taught it as a compulsion in the curriculum. But what makes it so groundbreaking? Let's find out!

Mischel called in a few preschoolers for an experiment. He presented each participant with a few marshmallow treats, placed neatly in front of them on a plate on the table. The preschooler was first asked a few basic questions like their name, age and school and then was told to wait as the researcher had to leave the room for a few minutes. However, the researcher, before leaving the room, told each preschooler that they had a choice to make. If the preschooler waited for the researcher to come back and didn't eat any of the marshmallows in front of them, they would get two. If they couldn't resist, they must ring a bell which would bring the researcher back into the room immediately. However, here's the catch. Then the preschooler will only be given one marshmallow to eat. A simple experiment so far, right?

However, the astonishing thing to note here was that not all preschoolers were able to resist the chewy sweetness. They evaluated the pros and cons of getting one instead of two if they rang the bell. Some were able to resist until the researcher returned to the room and some rang the bell sooner. The experiment was monitored by multiple researchers who tested the patience and self-control in the kids.

The most important finding was that when we were told to stay away from something, our urge to have it increased marginally. The satisfaction associated with it also increased. Before entering the room, no child had cravings for marshmallows. But when they were presented with some and specifically told to resist them, that is where things changed.

The same thing happens with us, too. Despite telling ourselves not to give in to a certain distraction or temptation, we become more eager than before to have it. For example, even if you tell yourself that you won't look at your social media accounts all day long or indulge in senseless browsing, it becomes so hard to abstain. But on any other given day, when engrossed in something we passionately feel committed to, we hardly ever think about going online or posting something.

The experiment also helped the researchers understand how humans delay gratification for a greater reward. They explained it using the hot and cool system in our bodies. The system allows us to see why we can resist temptations at times and why not at other times. The hot system is concerned with instant gratification without worrying about the consequences. It is like drinking the first sip of a fizzy drink, the first bite of the cake or a candy popped into the mouth. The hot system handles spontaneous as well as reflexive trigger responses.

The cool system, on the other hand, involves cognitive thinking. It entails deep compression over actions, sensations, goals and feels and takes more time in calculating the pros and cons of our actions. Such as not giving in to the temptation of a fizzy drink because it has too much sugar, which isn't good for your health.

If you need a more apt definition of the hot and cool system, think of them as the two angels on your shoulders. One is deemed nice and the other, evil. One encourages us to abstain from bad things while the other encourages us to go for it. They both keep fighting over everything. Sometimes, good wins and other times, we finally give in. When that happens, the hot system overrides the cool and causes impulsive reactions. Some people rarely have that happen and for others, it is more common than usual.

But the study didn't stop there. Mischel went back to check on the preschoolers in their adolescence and noticed that the preschoolers that had resisted the temptation and waited for the researcher to return into the room had better academic scores. They were likely to handle stress better, plan wiser, and have higher SAT scores. They were also better at exhibiting self-control and focus without distractions.

Mischel, after four decades, again tracked down the preschoolers to see how they were doing in their professional lives and as predicted, the preschoolers that had resisted the temptation were more successful in their relationships and careers than those who hadn't. This proved that traits like self-control, discipline, and willpower remain persistent throughout one's life.

Chapter 3:

What If Procrastination Comes in the Way?

Procrastination is no less than a plague that we can't avoid. It spreads like a virus, is contagious and ensures that the victim fully suffers at its hands. By definition, it is the act of delaying, avoiding or postponing any necessary task by focusing on some other pleasure-inducing and sensation-seeking activity. The simplest example would be browsing the Internet and watching videos of cute kittens showing off their tiny paws instead of working on the more important, deadline-oriented project at hand. It is very easy to blame a lack of self-control or willpower but laziness is also to blame for it. There are several reasons why we procrastinate and ways it affects our productivity, and in this chapter we are going to be reviewing some of them so that we can put an end to this epidemic.

But before we do that, it is important to understand the role the human brain plays in it all.

The Science Behind Procrastination

According to science, procrastination occurs when two parts of the brain spark a fight in between them when given a certain unwanted, undesirable or boring task. These two parts are the limbic and prefrontal cortex. The limbic system in the brain is responsible for inducing pleasure and is usually an unconscious zone, whereas the prefrontal cortex is an evolved part of the brain responsible for all the internal planning that goes into the brain. The prefrontal cortex supports logic, rationality, and reasoning. The limbic system, not so much. So whenever, during the fight between the two, the limbic system wins, we end up putting off the task at hand for a later time or date. And when the prefrontal cortex wins, we end up doing what we are supposed to be doing. However, many other factors come into play. Although the limbic system offers temporary relief, it usually lasts for a short duration and ends with worry and anxiety in the end. We may get rid of the unpleasant feeling of doing something we don't feel like doing, but eventually, it will sneak up on us in the form of worry or even stress.

Another interesting thing about these two parts of the brain is that the limbic system is the most dominant area of the brain and is on auto-pilot mode. It is the same thing that signals us to pull our hand away from fire or seek higher ground when drowning. It is programmed to perform basic survival instincts. In simpler terms, it is aimed at offering instant gratification or repairing. So for one, you can stop putting all the blame on yourself because your limbic system plays a key role.

Conversely, the relatively newly-discovered prefrontal cortex helps you integrate information and make informed and well-devised decisions. It is the part that makes us human in the first place and separates us from the rest of the species. Sadly, its functioning isn't automatic which means that you have to make the effort to get it in gear. For instance, you will have to eliminate all distractions, get into the working mindset, have all the required tools near you and finally, tell yourself to get back to work to start the prefrontal cortex's operations. The moment you lose the slightest focus from the task, your limbic systems regains control and you are drawn towards all sorts of things that promise instant gratification.

Can Procrastination be Good?

Ever since its discovery, procrastination has received a bad reputation. As humans, we all want to be the fastest, quickest, and the first one to ever perform something. We want to be the ones who get the most done in less time. Take races, for instance. The whole idea is who can finish the fastest. So, technically, procrastination shouldn't exist, correct? There should be no such thing if we are so focused on winning against everyone. Well, sympathizers of procrastination regard it as a good thing. But how does that link with our need to be the fastest? Hold your horses and continue reading. We promise to leave you with a connection.

People who think procrastination can be good give the following reasoning.

Procrastination helps you to manage delays.

One of the biggest perks, according to the sympathizers of procrastination, is that it helps us to learn how to manage delays. However, when they say that, they are talking about active procrastination and not passive procrastination. The former is considered good whereas the latter isn't, as it involves deliberately putting off things even when no distractions are around. For instance, sitting idle is passive procrastination. When you know that even if you put off things, you will manage to finish them before the set deadline, that (according to procrastinators) helps make you more creative and smart.

Procrastination helps you focus on the MITs.

Most important tasks (MITs) are tasks that are of the highest urgency and importance. Luckily, when we procrastinate and are left with less time, we can prioritize things better. We can focus on the things of the highest priority and accomplish them first. Once you have them done and dusted, you can move on to the less important ones or delay doing them if you want.

Better decisions are a reward of procrastination.

When we have many things to do and ample time on hand, we often take up more than we can handle. We think that we will have them accomplished, which can be wrong. We often accept chores and tasks that aren't ours to handle or we find ourselves ill-equipped to perform. This can cause stress, which further affects our productivity. However, when we are running short on time, we only stick to things we should be doing and don't indulge in unnecessary work, which results in making better decisions.

Procrastination kick-starts prioritization.

As stated earlier, a shortage of time can help us prioritize better. This allows the performer to eliminate all those tasks they deem unnecessary or not worth the time and effort.

Active procrastination can help you get more done.

Active procrastination means you put off something for later but don't waste the present time. Instead, you do something else. This can be effective when you don't feel like working on something and instead of just sitting idle, you stay engaged in other less urgent but important things. You can make time for a dozen things on your to-do list and as the time gradually passes, you move on to the task you had delayed earlier. That way, you will still have achieved something and not just wasted your time away.

Procrastination helps the mind to process better.

It is a stated fact that even when we aren't consciously thinking about something in the present, your subconscious is still thinking about it (James-Enger, 2009). We also know that the more time we indulge in thinking about something, chances are the more creative we can be. This is why the need to revise things comes highly recommended. The more time we spend delaying something, the more time we have to be creative and inventive. Therefore, in a way, it can be said that postponing or avoidance can lead to a burst of creativity.

And finally, it can be beneficial for your health, too.

Active procrastination is rarely accompanied by worry or stress. The more we get done in the meantime, the more accomplished and happier we feel. Research further reveals that people who indulge in active procrastination experience low-stress levels, have healthy self-efficacy and exhibit fewer avoidant tendencies (Chun Chu & Choi, 2010).

Tomorrow - The Word We Are So Obsessed With

If you have ever wondered why you procrastinate or can't seem to understand why you do it so often, below are some of the most common reasons why we feel so tempted to put off things for a later time or date. While going through the list, try to be reflective. We want you to be honest and identify the reasons that lead you to procrastinate so that you can work on those weaknesses and improve productivity and ultimately, your chances of succeeding in life.

Abstract Goals

One of the most common reasons we all procrastinate is because our goals are quite vague. We want to succeed but we don't even know what that means. We want to improve our productivity but we have no blueprint of how we are going to do that. Every goal needs a direction and drive. Lacking either means the goal isn't assertive. Goals without clearly-defined missions are no goals at all. Your goals should have some well-devised steps and a destination. You can't simply spend your life trying to lose weight but never know why you want to do so, so badly. You need more than just, "get fit" as a goal. In this case, you must have a reason to do so, set a date to start with, and have the means to achieve it. A goal that states, "I want to lose weight so that my confidence spikes high," seems more compelling. Add to that a date or day like, "I will start from Monday onwards" and, "I need to join a gym or get a new bike or hike hills" and you have a clearly-defined goal to begin with. Chances are, if you create each goal in this manner, you will be much more likely to stick with it.

A Better Future

Another reason so many individuals enjoy procrastinating is that they are hoping for a better or more attractive offer or course of action. The attractiveness of the current goal or task might not seem so tempting at the moment, so you deliberately wait for a better time. Think of it as a sale to buy a new pair of boots, even though you need them in the present too. This might not seem so hazardous but it can make one a persistent procrastinator. This sort of mindset doesn't work for everything and sometimes, things must be done in the present. If one becomes a persistent procrastinator, they may never end up following up on their intended plan.

Aiming for Perfectionism

Many people procrastinate because they aim for perfection in everything. Perfection doesn't exist and those aiming for it, never feel satisfied. Therefore, the goal should be to aim for progress instead. When we become too cautious of making errors, we may end up giving up on taking action altogether, which doesn't get them anywhere.

Other times, some individuals are so insecure about their work that they keep going back and revising an already-perfect draft or plan. When they do so, they always keep finding flaws in it and end up feeling more insecure than before. This can not only give birth to procrastination but also make one lose confidence in their abilities and skills.

Fear of Criticism

Constructive or negative – some people just don't take criticism well. They feel judged and evaluated. The fear of it can make one avoid putting in the work or doing it wholeheartedly because they have this idea that no matter how well they perform, they will still be scrutinized. This fear leads to them postpone working on something.

Waiting for the Thrill

Sometimes, the reason many people put off things until the very last minute is so that they can experience the pressure and challenge it promises. Some people get such a high when they feel challenged. It is just how they see themselves working their best. So they deliberately waste time so that they can feel the nerves when the time crunch comes in swiftly.

Getting Distracted

Getting distracted or distractibility can be described as the inability to stay focused on something or maintain a certain level of focus. The more distracted you are, either internally or due to external factors around you, the more likely you are to procrastinate. Therefore, it is so important to stay focused and avoid falling prey to distractions.

Prioritization of Temporary Enjoyment

Another reason to procrastinate can be giving in to short-term or temporary emotions in the present. If we have the choice to go watch a movie we have been dying to watch or work on the financial report of the company, what seems more interesting? Even when you know you should be working on the report, you somehow convince yourself that you should go watch the movie and stay awake a few extra hours before bedtime to work on the report. You are willing to forgo something important for short-term enjoyment or pleasure. This is also known as short-term mood repair which takes one's mind off goals that align with their long-term success and submit to their present feelings or emotions.

Poor Energy Levels

Low energy levels can be another reason why people put off things for tomorrow. Poor energy levels mean you lack the physical, emotional or mental strength to complete a task and thus, delay doing it altogether. For example, if you had a tough time at work such as visiting the construction site, staying out in the heat all day or just running here and there on multiple floors of the office, you might not be tempted to go to the gym after work. You already feel low on energy, and going to the gym would only mean draining some more. Therefore, you put it off for tomorrow because you just can't deal with the strenuous workout with such depleting energy levels.

Zero Motivation

Sometimes, the reason we procrastinate so often is that the task at hand isn't related to our interests. We see it as something boring and therefore are unable to build that drive to get started with it. Motivation is a driving force to get things done. Without it, we might begin but will surely lose momentum later on. There are two types of motivation – intrinsic (from within) and extrinsic (external). Extrinsic motivation is harder to get along with as it involves orders or pressure. An example of this would be your partner pressuring you to take up dance classes along with them for their sister's big wedding. When motivation isn't intrinsic – coming from within – it is very hard to go along. So to say that you are likely to procrastinate when forced or pressured into doing something makes complete sense as you don't feel motivated from the start.

You (*barely*) Make it Every Time

Some people pull off their best work under immense pressure. They claim that their mind works best when challenged or excited and thus, they deliberately put things off until the last minute. But there is no guarantee that this approach towards work will always produce the best work. You might have gotten lucky 95% of the time with it, but the remaining 5% is also important and failing at completing it means a bad reputation. So, even when you have been making it right before the clock struck the deadline, aim for getting done with it earlier, as it might not work all the time.

Sluggishness

You are simply lazy! That's it! You simply don't feel like doing something so you keep delaying it until the very last minute. Being lazy isn't bad, however if it becomes habitual and the delays in work lead to an ill reputation, then you need to reassess your goals and avoid procrastinating.

Anxiety

Have you ever felt incredibly anxious about something? Perhaps it was minutes before you had to deliver a big presentation or head in for an interview or meet someone for a blind date. You must have had those funny jitters in your stomach that won't leave for a good amount of time. You weren't able to think, sit in one spot or just keep your nerves under control. This happens when we feel anxious about something. Anxiety is another reason why people procrastinate. They feel so anxious about the task that they don't know where to start. If this is the reason why you have been pushing things to a later date and not addressing the elephant in the room, then you need to understand that avoidance won't make it go away. You will have to address it eventually. So take some time to think about how you are going to manage it and then approach it more confidently.

Task Aversion

If you don't like the task you have been assigned then you will delay starting on it. Task aversion is a very real thing and gets the best of many individuals. We are all driven by our passions. We jump to get started with something we truly love doing. For instance, if you have always been a people person or enjoy social interactions, then you will be more willing and excited about being on the team that organizes the company's picnics and annual events than on the team that bookkeeps. Procrastination occurs when we feel averse to a task. Some tasks are just plain boring, tedious or frustrating. Sometimes the individual believes that they lack the competence required or that it is simply too difficult. So they keep delaying it and engaging themselves elsewhere.

Fear of Failing

We have all been there. Remember when we would wake up in the middle of the night, thinking we had gotten a D on our test? The fear of failing can be another factor that prevents task completion and leads to procrastination. Knowing that you will eventually fail at it is highly demotivating. No one wants to feel discouraged or incompetent. How afraid we feel also depends on various factors such as how important or high-priority the task is. The more important it is, the more the chances of procrastination. Next, one's lack of self-esteem and confidence in their abilities can also render one afraid of starting something. People with such traits are more likely to procrastinate as opposed to those who are confident and decisive.

You Don't Value Commitments

It should be worrying that you take more time than needed for any given task. There is no point accomplishing something in two weeks that should have been done within a week. If you are poor at estimating the amount of time needed to fulfill a commitment, you may fall prey to procrastination. It is always relaxing to know that you have an ample amount of time. However, more time doing something is equivalent to less work done. If your goal is to increase productivity, you might need to work on this.

Indecisiveness

Some people also procrastinate because they are unable to make sensible decisions promptly. They overthink things which leads to delays in the commencement of things and ultimately, their end as well. The reasons for indecisiveness can be manifold. For example, when presented with many choices, it can be hard to choose one. A classic example of this can be picking a movie or TV show on Netflix when you have the time for it. Another reason can be not having a course of action or engagement to get started with. This results from a lack of planning. Then, the inability to make decisions can also be due to a lack of purpose or priority.

Sometimes people also fail to reach a conclusion when they are presented with multiple choices that all look the same. Ever gone shopping for tiles for your bathroom? You know what we mean! And finally, when one thinks that the decision is crucially important and affects the lives of many, they might lay it off until later to take some time to think about the pros and cons. However, what they fail to realize here is that every time we are met with a choice and we think about it, our mental resources deplete. The more choices we have, the higher the rate of depletion. A lack of mental focus is another reason that breeds procrastination as the individual keeps on postponing it for the time when they feel mentally-relaxed.

Lack of Control

A lack of control is another reason for procrastination. When we think that the outcomes aren't in our control, we lose interest. Even when we eventually do it after delaying it, we don't give our best effort. This perceived locus of control where the individual feels that their effort won't be appreciated or change the outcome of things makes them procrastinate.

From Procrastination to Productivity – The Leap of Faith

Now that we have identified the root causes of procrastination, it is time we move ahead to finding solutions that help us overcome it. One important thing that you must know here is that it isn't hard to form new habits. It takes a mere 30 days for us to learn a new one. This also means that we can get rid of the old, weakening and bad habits if we want to. New habits can become a part of you in no time.

Below are some of the most practical and doable ways to avoid falling into the trap of procrastination and let nothing get in the way of you and your success.

Adhere to Deadlines

Considering you have already created some, the first step is to strictly abide by the deadlines set, even if that means staying late for one day and working tirelessly the next. Deadlines help us follow a pattern and manage any delays happening in the middle. Deadlines also help us stay focused and not lose enthusiasm. When we know we will have to finish by a certain date from the get-go, we plan and prioritize accordingly. This enhances our productivity and prevents us from procrastinating.

You can also subdivide the actual deadline into shorter ones. For instance, if you have been given a task that needs to be completed in ten days, you can set a deadline for the fifth day to reach half of it. This comes in handy with authors and journalists who write a lot and are constrained by a deadline. They set a goal for each day and the end of the day serves as the deadline.

When breaking down deadlines, aim to keep them short. Deadlines that are too far-stretched can lead to procrastination and avoidance. The sooner the date of submission or completion, the higher the urgency to complete it.

Break Down Big Goals into Smaller Ones

It is impossible to achieve everything overnight, so don't let procrastination take you there. You must work consistently, even when working slowly. You must aim to achieve something to show as progress at the end of each day. However, when working on big projects or long-term goals, it is easy to lose momentum and drive. Every task requires a certain level of focus and commitment and when you lack either, it hampers your productivity. When we are handed more than we can handle, it is easy to lose track and become confused. Big or important tasks also come with the added pressure of failure and stress. But all of this can be avoided if one just learns to break down big tasks into smaller ones. Each step of the process can serve as an individual goal on its own. The idea is to break it down in achievable milestones that aren't too difficult or overwhelming. Set a time for each short goal and accomplish each task one at a time. Gradually, make your way from the first task to the second and so on. The little bouts of encouragement and achievement will keep you focused, happy, motivated, and keep the momentum going.

Set Rewards

There are countless books on parenting that preach that the best way to instill a good habit or get rid of a bad one is positive reinforcement.

It is so effective that the same strategy applies to your pets, too. Positive reinforcement includes the setting of some form of tangible or intangible reward for the successful completion of a task. For example, rewarding your child with ice cream after dinner if they clean their room or letting your dog pick their favorite snack if they stop defecating in their kennel.

The same technique can be applied in business settings and daily life as well. Rewards are known to boost productivity, improve focus and enhance motivation. When the goal is to avoid delaying something, rewards can work wonders and keep us working. The best thing about rewards is that they don't always have to be tangible. It can be intangible like self-appreciation, longer break times or some time to browse social media. The key is to set rewards that you are most passionate about so that you may experience a higher level of motivation. So when procrastination does strike, you can shush it away by reminding yourself of what awaits ahead.

Work Short Hours

Picture this: you started on a task in the morning. You were all pumped up in the start but as the day wears on, you find yourself losing interest. It wasn't just the presence of tempting distractions or the lack of planning. You simply lost heart and instead of performing better, found yourself underperforming. This happens when we work on one thing for several hours at a time. The mind becomes saturated and can't take anymore. It is rendered unable to think or process the same patterns of information it had been for the past hours. Therefore, it is essential to give the mind some time to cool off and keep working hours short. The best way to do so is the introduction of short breaks in between tasks. Breaks allow the mind to come out of the trance and become revitalized. When we do that, even the most tedious of tasks will seem doable and you won't worry about procrastinating. Furthermore, keep in mind that while you are taking the break, avoid thinking about the task. That will only lead to further loss of motivation and take all the fun and enjoyment out of the task. And we all know what happens when we aren't fully committed or driven to do something – procrastination takes over!

Chapter 4:

Time Management, Productivity

and Success - What's the Link?

Did you know workplace interruptions cost companies approximately $588 billion due to lost productivity in the US each year (Brown, 2015)? Productivity is the essence of being productive. It is about bringing something to the table. It is about putting in effort to fulfill a certain goal. It is about being able to perform and be actionable. But sometimes, despite our best intentions and effort, we fail to be productive. Yes, we have all had one of those days where we can't do anything no matter how much time and energy we put in. Our mind just doesn't wrap around anything or stay focused. These are what we call barriers to productivity and they can be abundant. Since we have already discussed some of the biggest ones in the chapter earlier, we are going to stick with the ones we haven't discussed already and look at the negative impact they have on our ability to perform in our best capacity.

Barriers to Productivity

Disengagement from Work

Research from the AXA PPP healthcare revealed that 42% of small-business employees blame disinterest or the lack of enjoyment at the job as one of the primary factors for the lack of productivity. The more advanced technological means get, the more disinterested we become with our work. Despite having the best productivity-enhancing apps and time-tracking metrics, our rate of productivity is declining overall. Even more surprising is the fact that two-thirds of businesses DO track productivity. But is it also understandable that the more monotonous the work, the poorer our productivity? Other than disinterest, many other influences hinder productivity. These include:

Poor Communication

Face-to-face communication has become more fragmented than ever. Although calling someone and having a video chat takes less than a minute, unlike before, communications have become more ambiguous. They are less contextual, send mixed messages and can harm one's productivity. Poor communication costs companies millions every year as things get delayed when plans haven't been coordinated well or have discrepancies that require reworking. Take the marketing industry, for example. How many times has it happened that the client rejects the design sent and the designer has to rework from the start, wasting valuable time and resources? If communication has become so transparent, shouldn't they be able to get it done right the first time? It is no secret that the more revisions we are made to perform, the poorer our productivity gets.

Miscommunication, another variant of poor communication, is an even bigger evil. Miscommunication can occur on the same level, too. Employees may lack the required information and fear asking for clarity, resulting in the poor quality of work and wasted time and energy. Weak communication channels between the employee and the employer can also lead to a decline in one's productivity and disrupt the work culture and relationships.

Poor Working Environment

We all work best in different work conditions. Some require pin-drop silence to focus whereas others crave noise and thus take their work outside the walls of the office and into cafes or malls. They seem to enjoy the chaos and know the art of drowning out all those noises and still be able to avoid distractions. Not having a suitable working environment, be it with the wrong people, poor lighting or just close spaces, if we feel uncomfortable being in our chair, then it can hinder our productivity. Therefore, we have to ensure that workplaces are free of all sorts of clutter so that we can focus better and ultimately perform better. We have to create a space that doesn't allow distractions to overpower us. This means we have to create a safe distance between us and our technological gadgets, too. Having a TV playing in your room all the time isn't going to do wonders for your productivity, it is only going to bring it down by constantly distracting you with the vibrant colors and the breaking news sections. Similarly, the wrong room temperature can also create problems with your productivity. If you feel hot or cold every time someone switches on/off the AC nearest to you, it can irritate you and make you lose your focus.

Cluttered Workstations

Similar to the point above, having a clutter-filled desk or working station is another barrier to productivity. One keeps breaking the momentum of work looking through the clutter or getting tangled in charging wires. It is important to have everything in place before you even begin.

Demotivating Benefits

Not long ago, the only thing that excited people about applying for a job was if it aligned with their current passions or not. They were okay getting paid less as long as they were able to do the things they enjoyed doing. This gave rise to unpaid internships and everyone just felt the need to associate themselves with organizations they felt strongly about. They were willing to put in the hours, do the extra work, pay for their commute and still come home feeling happy. But not anymore.

Today, people follow their passions less and better money more. They are willing to make the switch as soon as a better opportunity comes by. There is little integrity and loyalty to the company. But the employees aren't to blame here – the management is. They don't offer anything tempting enough that it would make the employees think twice before making the switch. The bonuses are overdue, the appraisals seem biased and the work culture isn't good either. All of this also leads to poor productivity in the workplace as the employee is only interested in getting their paycheck and not about how good or bad the company is doing. They are unwilling to do more or go beyond the call of duty to help their company prosper. What employers need to do here is offer exciting incentives that the employees can't resist. Demanding incentives is the right of the employees as it is a tell-tale sign that they want to be appreciated and acknowledged for all that they do. If they don't feel either, one can't expect them to perform at their best.

Lack of Training

Lack of training is another reason why some individuals face difficulty in staying productive. Not all employees join the organization with an ideal set of skills. Many things are learned on the job. We may excel in some skills but not all, which is why we remain a student all our lives. And with how fast the work dynamics are changing, training and development have become a crucial department in nearly all big enterprises. The gaps and lack of experience can be worked upon in the form of training. However, when the company fails to provide it, it can become a barrier to productivity. When individuals lack the knowledge or skills to perform a certain task, they can't be expected to perform their best or remain productive. They are likely to make errors or be unable to finish the given task.

Time Management and Productivity

You might get sidetracked by external influences such as distractions, staff chatter, unexpected chores, meetings, email pop-ups, and social media. All of these are things that you aren't hired to do and thus, wasting too much time on these is against ethics, too. Did you know, many of these personal tasks take up at least 40% of our day's work? This was found when a management software company called Workfront decided to survey more than 2,010 workers performing an 8-hour working shift every day (Renzulli, 2019). The survey's primary focus was to identify how much time the workers did the work they were paid for and what amount of time was going unaccounted for annually. 40% equals approximately three hours per eight-hour shifts which leaves us with only five hours of productive work. This 60% or five hours further get divided into the following.

- 16% of the time is spent on checking and responding to emails.
- 12% of the time is spent on performing administrative tasks.
- 10% of the time, we are indulged in useful meetings, whereas 8% of the time, we are dragged through unwanted ones.
- 8% of the time is spent on interruptions and the remaining 6% of the time is utilized elsewhere.

But then again, there is this one person who, despite all these interruptions, can get everything off their to-do list. They are always submitting work before deadlines, coming up to presentations all prepped and delivering the best ideas that can only be a result of extensive research and market trend analysis. So how are they doing it and why can't we? They have the same hours in a day to work. Then how are they more productive than us?

This intrigued a senior lecturer, Robert C. Pozen at the MIT Sloan School of Management. He surveyed over 20,000 people across six continents to have a broader understanding of how some people were able to achieve more and some weren't. Despite common belief, they weren't working any extra or long hours, they were just working smarter. What does that even mean? Working smarter means getting the most important things out of the way first and then using the leftover time to do miscellaneous or less important tasks. They were planning better and prioritizing even better. This research was later published in the Harvard Business Review and helped change the mindset of many managers and employees worldwide (Pozen & Downey, 2019).

Professionals who prefer working smarter over working harder scored better in the survey. They had the habit of planning and setting priorities accordingly. They had developed strategies and techniques that helped them sort through a large amount of information and understand the needs of other employees, too.

What comes recommended to becoming productive are a few habits that you can easily learn and adapt, concluded the findings of the published survey. These include:

- Revising daily action plans and rescheduling something important accordingly.
- Have everything planned a night before so that you can go to work already knowing what to do.
- Learn to prioritize things according to their urgency and importance.
- Use calendars, to-do lists, and planners to jot down important events, messages or tasks.
- Whenever you're starting something, spend the first five minutes outlining the process and how you will proceed with each step.
- Create a logical order of doing things so that everything stays in flow. You shouldn't have to go back or skip a few steps to solve the current task.
- Allot a specific time to check the screens of your phones and computers. Don't do it every other minute.
- Don't reply to all emails as they come. Prioritize them based on who sent it and the urgency of response.
- Keep meetings short and direct. All the employees attending it should already have a memo a day before the meeting so that they are aware of what will be discussed.

Time Management, Happiness, and Increased Productivity

Our mood has a significant effect on productivity as well. When we aren't stressed or angry, we can focus better and thus, be more productive. This idea was further explored by the author of the bestseller *Stumbling on Happiness*, Daniel Gilbert. According to Mr. Gilbert, a wandering or unfocused mind is neither happy nor productive. He argues that since we are so prone to multitasking, we rarely get things done timely and don't make the most of 45% of our waking time. When we keep switching between tasks or thinking about them all simultaneously, we allow ourselves to wander in different directions. This form of wandering reaps nothing productive and adds to our levels of stress, making us feel unhappy.

Therefore, to be happier and productive, we need to manage whatever time we have at its best. We have to ensure that we don't do any such thing that gives our minds the chance to wander off and trigger stress. According to one study published in the Journal of Happiness, people who can manage their free time well enjoy a better quality of life (Wang, Kao, Huan, & Wu, 2011).

How can we make that happen? Laura Vanderkam has the answer. She writes in her book *What the Most Successful People Do at Work: A Short Guide to Making Over Your Career* that successful people value their time like capital. They are, at all times, conscious about where they are spending their time. They have chosen to stay wealthy and therefore, spend most of their time doing things that take them closer to their goal.

Cal Newport also seems to have the same advice. The renowned author of *Deep Work* and the owner of the Study Hacks Blog, Cal thinks that the reason some people achieve success in their lives so easily is that they have the habit of scheduling every working day. It seems daunting at first, but once you develop the habit of scheduling every minute of it, you will notice how easy it gets once you have everything figured out. While you're at it, you also come to terms with any deadlines or important dates you might have overlooked and add them to your to-do list. Additionally, when you assign limited time brackets for each task and already have another one scheduled ahead, you are less likely to procrastinate and will stay determined to complete it.

Time Management, Attention Span, and Productivity

Larry Rosen, a research psychologist and educator, studied the correlation between the attention span and productivity in students (Stringer, 2017). He wanted to know the effects of technology in the lives of students and if it was helping them accomplish things faster or not. However, when he gathered 260 middle school, high school, and university kids for an experiment, he found that the drawbacks of technology came disguised as benefit and were the cause of poor attention spans and the lack of focus in the kids. During the experiment, the participating students were asked to study at their home for 15 minutes. During those 15 minutes, the students' reactions were monitored. Rosen discovered that it took all the students less than 6 minutes to lose attention and switch to another task or distraction. These usually came in the form of a text, phone vibration, beep or an alert. He also noted that it wasn't just these alerts, but the students themselves picked up their electronic devices, with or without any notifications. Rosen argued that although technological advances were created to improve our learning and skills, they were doing the opposite. Not only did the students lose valuable time while checking their messages, but they also weren't productive. This meant that productivity was indirectly proportional to distractions. The more distraction-oriented the environment, the poorer the productivity. The poorer the productivity, the more time wasted.

It also pointed out that we couldn't multitask. If we thought we did, we were wrong. We only switched between tasks. The former task just became salient as we made the switch and when we came back to it, we lost some good time trying to remember where we were and then continue from there onwards.

Therefore, the goal should be to minimize distractions and increase our attention span. When our attention span increases, we will be less receptive to distractions and, hopefully, save time. The best way to do so is to set a time for social interactions. Start with taking breaks in between and checking the messages and alerts for a given amount of time and when the time is up, return to doing what you were with complete focus. Another way can be removing the distractions from the room altogether. If that is not possible, you might want to put them on silent for some time and keep them some distance from you.

Time Management, Distractions, and Productivity

Did you know that such a form of distraction caused our mind to become like the mind of someone smoking marijuana? According to one British study, workers suffer a great loss of IQ when distractions hit which is greater than the loss of IQ of an individual smoking pot.

Another research study carried out by TNS Research aimed at finding the role of constant disruptions in the form of emails and phone calls. The constant interruptions make one lose time, feel lethargic and reduce productivity. The survey included 1,100 Britons. During the survey, the following statistics emerged.

- Two out of three people check their phones for official messages when on holidays or during out of office hours.
- Half of them are quick to respond to emails and are likely to respond within the first hour of receiving them.
- One out of five people break off from social gatherings to respond to emails or phone calls outside of work hours.
- Nine of the people thought that coworkers who, during face to face interactions, tended to their messages were rude. All ten believed that it was unacceptable behavior and also a sign of poor efficiency and diligence.

Revealing these, we now understand that all of these can have a direct impact on our productivity and cause us to lose valuable time. Proper management of time, as well as the elimination of all such interruptions outside of working hours, should be top priority. One shouldn't be obliged to respond to messages that are received after work hours and the people who do so shouldn't be appreciated more than others or seen as high achievers. Companies should invest in properly training their employees and staff members to make the most of the working hours and hold back on messages and emails when received outside of work. Another important reason to do so is that when people remain so engulfed in just their work, their mental sharpness and presence of mind suffer. They start to lose interest in other things and regard them as unimportant. However, not everything that doesn't involve work is unimportant. Therefore, one must always aim to find a work-life balance.

Productivity and Success

This seems to be one of the most important correlations that the book is based on. Are productivity and success related? If so, are they dependent or independent and what factors can influence the rate? More importantly, what role does time management play in all this? But before we get to all that, we need to dissect the term success. What is success? Is there some universal definition? Does it only mean accomplishments related to one's work? Is it achievable? Are there some metrics to track it? Is it constant?

Success can mean different things to different people. However, ironically, whenever we hear someone being labeled as successful, our mind automatically pictures someone with luxurious cars, a big house, private yachts, fancy watches, and suits. But if it means just the attainment of wealth, then it is quite stern.

Webster's dictionary provides the following definition: the accomplishment of an aim or purpose.

Now, if we note, the word purpose or aim seems important. But not everyone aims to attain wealth. Some just want fame, love, or to be seen for who they are. They want to follow their passion as that is what serves as a purpose to them. Some want to spend their lives helping and providing for others. That seems to be their goal or aim. So, the first thing that we need to understand is that a purpose can be anything and the accomplishment of that purpose is what real success is. In broader terms, it is something that makes one appreciate life and be happy.

Don't get us wrong. We are in no tussle with the associated definition of the term with wealth and riches, however, we would rather wish to explore the many variations it can have. It should mean achievement, triumph or accomplishment of any kind and not just wealth. Because neither of the two definitions we discussed above even mentioned the words money, luxury, or wealth. So, there is a possibility that someone who doesn't have a mansion can also be successful without a fortune. Moreover, there have been no standardized means to measure success. Then again, success doesn't have a time frame either. One may feel successful one day and unsuccessful the next. Success should be determined by what we can achieve in a single day. It should come down to whether we can live up to the aims and objectives set for the day or not. This was further backed by Andy Frisella, a famous influencer and podcaster. According to Andy, success is the pursuit of fulfillment of an individual's true potential (Frisella, 2017). Let's understand it by breaking it down. Andy suggests that becoming successful at something involves actively seeking improvement and tapping into one's true or full potential. This is only possible when one constantly works towards the long-term goals they have for themselves. Working constantly involves working every day and making the most of the waking hours available for progress. So, it DOES come down to how the time is managed and what is done in that time. If we are not making progress every day and accomplishing our daily goals, then we are not working towards becoming successful. On the other hand, when we are working half-heartedly and not in our full capacity, we are also limiting our chances of success. Therefore, success can be defined as a combination of both productivity and efficient time management as these two seem to be the most crucial factors in all of the definitions stated in the section.

Thus, the correlation we started looking for had been right here in front of our eyes all the time. We were just a little late to crack it.

Furthermore, there has been quite a buzz about these three being codependent on one another. How so, you may ask? For one, we know that time is a valuable resource because Benjamin Franklin told us so. Then, Brian Tracy notched it up saying that it is irreplaceable and perishable. Knowing that time management is the essence of productivity and success allows us to view it from a different perspective and value it. We know that we can spend the whole day watching TV and not going to work or doing chores, but we don't. Even when, on weekends, we have the opportunity to do so, we engage ourselves in any pending work that remains. Why? Because, subconsciously, we know that the time we spend watching TV won't come back. So we spend it doing the things that matter more and leave us with a sense of accomplishment. But this only happens when we begin to view time as a finite source and cherish every minute of it. And why not? After all, it does the following for us.

Time Management Leads to Improved Health

When we feel fit physically and emotionally, we perform better. There is no need for a research study to understand that. Our chances of performing better enhance. What many people don't know is that too much stress can kill, literally (Hartz-Selley, 2014). Chronic stress is often linked to increased heart rate, blood pressure, cancer, cirrhosis of the liver, and lung ailments. Stress affects the brain directly and becomes the reason for blood sugar imbalances. This reduces our immunity which means that it takes longer to heal.

Time management and stress management work in unison. When time is managed wisely, you feel more in control. When you feel more in control, you can perform at a better pace and with focus. This prevents any last-minute surprises and deadlines are met on time. When you feel healthy, you feel more prepared to handle anything.

Time Management Helps you Accomplish More

When time crunches are your biggest pet peeves, it is imperative that you stay focused and eliminate distractions. Elimination of distractions means more work is done at the end of the day, which ultimately means reaching closer to your goals. Isn't that the actual definition of success? Therefore, with proper time management, success becomes a reality. It happens because one knows what they want and thus, don't lose the tempo. You are in a better position to avoid getting distracted and get through all the set tasks for the day in an eloquent manner.

When taking control of your time you can improve your ability to focus and eliminate distractions, which in turn will make you more productive (Maddox, 2019).

Time Management Reduces Re-work

Thanks to the principles of time management, when we begin to manage our time efficiently, there are reduced incidences of re-work and errors. But that doesn't mean that time management will make you a perfectionist, it will just help you fill in those gaps and loops that you often fail to notice when managing your time poorly. This happens when you have a to-do list or action plan in hand with each task assigned a set time. When you know exactly how much time each task requires and have all the necessary steps laid out, there is little room left for redundancies.

Time Management Improves Decision Making

When it comes to making important decisions at the last minute, many people feel pressured. The pressure can lead to one panicking and becoming anxious, and important information may get mulled over. When time is managed efficiently, there is little pressure to worry about, which means you can relax and analyze all the information you need to make an informed decision.

Time Management Boosts Reputation

Tell us this: what will others think of you if you are always the last one to show up and or keep missing deadlines? Your reputation will surely take a toll and your dream to become successful will remain just that.

No one likes to work with someone unreliable and flaky. When you manage time efficiently, you keep showing up on time, stay on schedule and have everything wrapped up before the deadline – a quality that many employers cherish in their subordinates.

Time Management Leaves you with Free Time

Although time management doesn't magically increase the hours in a day, it helps you strategically make the most of it. When you spend your designated working hours doing work, you are left with some leisure time in the end. This is the free time you can spend however you like. You get a chance to organize the clutter on the station, go through your email folders, make personal phone calls or go home and spend time with your family. This is a great way to de-stress yourself and also know that you have accomplished all that was planned for the day.

Finally, the one reason why you need to seriously start thinking about managing your time is that Belinda Weaver, in her book, labels poor time management as the shortcut to hell, and none of us would like to end up there!

Chapter 5:

Habits of Successful Time

Managers

Here's the thing: you won't learn to manage time overnight. No one does, not even the people you look up to for inspiration. Even your most favorite idols made mistakes but learned from them. They started even poorer than you and look where they are right now. We are talking about people like Benjamin Franklin, Maya Angelou, Oprah Winfrey, Steve Jobs or Albert Einstein. They all had to face the toughest of times, challenge the status quo, and stay focused on their dreams. They followed their passions, took their sweet time to give everything their 100% and become legends. Despite coming from different backgrounds, ethnicities, households, and generations, they all had one thing in common. They valued time. They didn't waste it on senseless friendships or meaningless relationships. Instead, they devoted their time to making things happen. Things that changed the world for the better. It is thanks to them that we can enjoy many luxuries in life and technological advancements.

If they did it, so can you. It seems too dramatic to even quote, but this is a fact. They had much less than we have today. Many of them didn't have the Internet or come from wealthy families supporting them. They were self-made because they knew what they wanted and they went after it without shame. Of course, there were obstacles they had to face, but they had it all planned. They knew from the very beginning that what they were setting themselves up for wasn't going to be easy. But they aimed to stay productive and walked the talk!

So if you are going to start, it better be today. Aim to be productive so that success finds you the same way it found them. Learn to manage your time better. It will be a lengthy process to begin with, but at least you will be on the right path. Since you will be developing many new habits along the way, it is only wise to do a quick self-assessment of where you currently are. The goal is to help you identify all those behaviors and habits that you need to enhance and pay attention to and also those that you need to avoid or give up.

Time Management Personality Types

Learn which personality most resonates with you so that you can figure out the behaviors and actions you need to work on and become better at managing the valuable resource that is time.

Are You a Firefighter?

Who, according to you, is a firefighter? Isn't it the person who runs in the direction of the crisis when everyone else seems to be fleeing from it? If you are someone like that who rushes to the scene and makes things better, is considered reliable and hates wasting time, then that makes you a firefighter. Your working style may not be the most ideal as you are always running here and there and causing chaos in the lives of others, but your ultimate goal is to make the most of whatever available time you have on your hands. This is a quality that many find attractive and worthy. You like taking risks but most of them are calculated.

However, there is only one drawback with the firefighter personality. Sometimes, they are so immersed in everything in front of them that they mistake not so urgent tasks as being urgent as well. There are always some things that can be put off for another time or delegated, but since they act like the doers, they have the habit of investing their time in everything, even when it isn't urgent.

Are you a Multitasker?

Are you someone who can handle a phone call and also sign some important documents after reading them simultaneously? If so, then your time management style is what we call a multitasker. At first, it does seem like an amazing superpower to have, but it isn't so in the long run. Why? Because multitasking is more of a myth than reality. We only think we are multitasking but we are just switching between two things very quickly. This increases the chances of redundancies, which isn't a good trait to have. So if you have been thinking that with multitasking, you will be able to get most out of your to-do list finished, you need to think again. You may have made mistakes along the way that will need reworking. If that is correct, what is the point of saving time earlier when you have to waste it making the corrections, later?

Are You an Over-Committer?

Are you someone who says yes to everything and everyone all the time? If so, then you are someone we label as an over-committer. An over-committer is someone who has trouble with boundaries. They are people pleasers and always find themselves doing other's work over their own. All you need is to do is ask them for their help or invite them to something and they will never disappoint.

But that leaves them unable to fulfill their commitments, which is bad. They eventually suffer from a bad reputation and when it finally comes to doing their tasks, they are left exhausted. After all, there is only so much that you can do in a day.

Are You an Underestimator?

Are you someone who always finds themselves uttering the following words?

"I just need a few more minutes."

"I will wrap this up in ten minutes, tops."

"You will have the report on your desk any minute now."

An underestimator is someone who manages time poorly. They never meet the deadline and are often seeking extensions. They tell you that it will take just a few minutes but they won't show up until an hour later and waste others' time, too.

Underestimating time constraints doesn't harm others as much as it harms you. It pushes back all the things you had planned and is a result of procrastination. You are always asking others to cover up for you or accommodate you later in their schedules. That doesn't make you seem like the reliable guy here, does it? So stop playing catch up and prioritize deadlines.

Are You a Perfectionist?

Obsession with perfectionism isn't healthy. Although you should always aim to give your 110% to every commitment, adhering to unrealistic expectations or setting the bar too high for yourself can be detrimental. You keep going back, making amends to an already perfect thing which makes you lose valuable time. If this sounds like you, then you must also have a hard time with deadlines, correct? Because everything seems like it can be improved and perfected. But ask yourself this: is there any end to perfectionism? Will you ever be happy with something you did the first time and not try to upstage it later?

Perfectionists are often too exhausted working on the same thing. There comes a point when their mind just stops concocting more ideas and that is when they realize they have invested more time in something that it deserved.

Are You a Wild Procrastinator?

Are you someone who deliberately pushes things until the last minute just so that you can enjoy the thrill of the challenge? If yes, then that makes you a wild procrastinator. Being a procrastinator that likes procrastinating is setting themselves up for a hit or miss kind of situation. You might think that doing so results in some of the most creative ideas coming to your mind, but it won't work all the time. Are you willing to sabotage your reputation over some thrill that gets you all sweaty, causes anxiety and wastes time?

As reported by Psychology Today, procrastinators have a weakened immune system. They also battle with insomnia and their mental state only worsens as the deadline approaches. They eat less, spend hours in front of the computer, and don't sleep well. All these unhealthy habits can leave a lifelong impact on your wellbeing.

Successful People and How They Manage Time

It is no secret that everyone starts at the bottom, but with proper guidance, healthy habits and some sane thinking, people can get where they want to be. Below are examples of some of the greatest minds in history, the famed inventors, inspirational celebrities and successful entrepreneurs who made it big because they valued time and learned to make the most of it. You will be astonished to note how incorporating just a few basic habits in your daily life can take you far and pave the way for your success. So if you need some inspiration from the gurus and masters of time, take a look below!

Benjamin Franklin

Benjamin Franklin had a very strict and rigid habit. Before the end of the day, he always took out the time to write down a summary of all the things he had accomplished that day. He even had a fixed time during the night when he asked himself what good he had done that day. He also summarized all the frustrations, roadblocks and obstacles that came in the way of doing things so that whenever he felt stuck, he could go back and see how he overcame them. Creating a recap of your day helps you plan your next day better. If you feel that you failed to live up to your expectations, then you will be motivated to get more done in the next day just so that you can stop feeling guilty. Not only does that save time with an action plan, but it also improves productivity with motivation and commitment.

Steve Jobs

The man who made Apple Inc. what it is today, Steve Jobs was all about a strong work ethic and commitment. He had this habit of looking at himself in the mirror each day and asking what he would want to do today if it were his last day on the planet. That helped him sort his top-most priorities without feeling guilty about pushing the others down. If the answer wasn't something he had planned for the day, he didn't mind changing the task and switching to what seemed more important. The idea is to do the things that are of most value instead of carelessly wasting time on unimportant things. This is possibly one of the most clichéd yet sensible pieces of advice to come from someone as great as Steve Jobs.

Warren Buffet

The most famous investor of all time, Warren Buffet is considered a man at the top of his game. With a huge following and managers and executives living by his wisdom and sensible advice, he strongly believes that a man creates his destiny with how much he is willing to work and sacrifice. He thinks that luck has little to do with success and that only those who truly crave it and are willing to make the effort are the ones who taste it. He greatly emphasized the importance of goal setting and teaches many of the best ways to prioritize and schedule tasks. There are tons of quotes one can look up to when in need of some inspiration, as his wisdom speaks for itself.

Evan Williams

The founder of Twitter and Blogger makes sure that he gets an ample amount of time to exercise and relax his mind during the day. This is ideal for those who feel like they are always drained of energy. Exercise can help pump up the lost adrenaline and make you feel more energetic. The higher your energy levels, the better your productivity will be. You will also be able to focus better and get things done in an efficient and error-free manner.

Barack Obama

Barack Obama values family times. He is all about sharing his morning with his wife and kids, helping her with breakfast and then helping his girls to get ready for school. He has a fixed exercise time as well as newspaper reading time before he heads off to his office at 9:00 a.m. sharp. He also makes time to have dinner with his family and then later delves into office business once again until bedtime. What his lifestyle teaches us is that one must always make time for the things that they value the most. To him, it is his family. For someone else, it can be their work or other commitments. The thing to note here is that you have to set priorities in life and ensure that no matter what, you always make time for them. You should make it a rule to spend time with the people or tasks that matter to you.

Another astonishing thing about Obama is that he doesn't care or worry too much about his clothes or meals. He calls them distractions and tries to stay away from them as much as possible. He hates decision fatigue, which means not wasting time on unimportant things and staying focused on the important ones so that the unimportant doesn't drain too much of your energy to think. This is a great piece of advice to look up to, as many of us are guilty of it. We spend too much time on menial things and when the time to think about something important comes, our mental capacity doesn't allow it. This can lead to poorly-made decisions over time.

Stephen King

The author of many world-famous fiction novels, Steven King keeps it real by having a decluttered space to work at. He firmly believes in the idea of persistent habits and what role they play in one's daily life. He chooses to begin his day in the same manner, every day. He starts with sitting down to work at a fixed time every morning, in his only chair while sipping on a glass of water. Then he carefully goes through his important documents, gets writing and plays the same music he listens to every day. He practices consistency as he thinks a man should have that in his life. Consistency eliminates distractions and helps one stay focused on the task at hand. That way, they don't end up wasting time gathering their thoughts or organizing the required resources.

Maya Angelou

Maya Angelou, like many dedicated writers, had rented a small sparse hotel room where only she, a bottle of sherry, a Bible and a deck of cards were allowed for the first half of the day. She was so determined to eliminate distractions and stay focused that she did nothing but write from 7:00 a.m. to 3:00 p.m. She staunchly believed in single-tasking. She knew it was the only effective way to get things done in a timely fashion. It was her sharp and adamant focus that led her to win some of the grandest and most prestigious awards such as the Tony, Pulitzer Award, and Grammy among others.

Bill Gates

The man who is considered as one of the most successful and humble human beings today, Bill Gates follows in the steps of Warren Buffet and has dedicated calendars but with a lot of blanks spaces. He believes that keeping some free or buffer space allows him to stay flexible and still be done with all the tasks on the list. He religiously believes in time management and is always prepared in case any unforeseen circumstances come up. The more "vacancies" he has on his calendars, the more time he has to work on things he is passionate about. This is what keeping a sane and sensible work-life balance looks like. You not only make time for your business but also enrich your soul with the things you are passionate about.

Ernest Hemingway

Ernest Hemmingway had the habit of waking up before the sun and writing until he was done with the things he had to say. During the afternoon, he would complete and touch upon any rough sketches and ideas that need improving and once done with that, he would begin planning for the next day. What Hemmingway had was incredible impulse control. Despite being surrounded by so many distractions, he never lost focus. Since he believed in attempting the most important task of the day first thing in the morning, he was always left with enough downtime to think and debate new ideas in his head. This is what controlled scheduling looks like and if we want to achieve a name as legendary as his, maybe we should start with the same, too.

Elon Musk

We already discussed a little about how frantic he is about time. It seems like the worst thing any of his employees can do is waste time. When hiring new people, he often hires them for their dedicated work ethic, even if they lack a graduate degree. He says that he is only interested in great ideas and they aren't bound by a degree, but rather one's creativity and sense of work. He hates the idea of unnecessary meetings and regards them as productivity killers. He is a fan of detailed emails and mostly uses platforms like Slack for communication with his colleagues and clients. If a meeting is important, he hands out each member a strict, time-crunched agenda and keeps it short during the time of the meeting. What we can learn from his lifestyle and overall work ethic is that he is more of a doer than just a talker. This is something you should aim for as well.

Tony Robbins

In his book, *The Ultimate Guide to Time Management*, the best-selling author and renowned business strategist suggests that one should value time the same way they value their money. After all, it is also a scarce resource and thus, should be treated like one. He proposes that the best way to make the most of the available time is by eliminating waste. He urges all of his followers to turn their wasteful time into productive time. To do so, he suggests repurposing time management in dead zones. If one fails to make time for something they want to push into their lifestyle, then carefully analyze the dead time zones such as commute or waiting for lines to incorporate those. For example, if you have a brilliant idea but are too busy to work on it further, use your commute time to further develop it.

Chapter 6:

Task Prioritization and Scheduling

Now that we have an idea of what the most famous world leaders and successful businessmen are doing, your intention to work smarter and be as productive as you can be must have grown. That's great, because in this chapter, we will start with how you can begin valuing time and making the most of it. Keep in mind, these aren't just tips but rather a complete mindset that we need to build first to become time-efficient.

Many of us struggle with multiple urgent requests daily. Something just finds us when we are most focused and makes us come out of that trance and do something else. Although it is less likely that it will happen every day, whenever it does, it changes the plan for the rest of the day. You find yourself in a fix because your to-do list has another task that needs fulfillment before the others.

So, the endless journey of playing catch-up begins as we are intent on getting everything off the list. However, this comes down to whether we have prioritized work formerly or not. For instance, you may have all the to-do tasks listed, but are they sorted in a sequence? If not, then that is what you need to do. This is where prioritizing and scheduling comes in.

There are two methods of ensuring that any upsets don't cause stress or leave you with more unfinished tasks. They help you to stay on track and keep moving forward with what had already been planned earlier – urgent or not urgent. It allows you to become proactive rather than reactive and increases your productivity exponentially. Since we will be touching a little on each subject individually, let's begin with prioritization and the techniques you can use to manage your limited time better.

The first thing you need is the creation of a to-do list that has everything mapped out. This includes the tasks that you plan on doing, the steps each task will take, the amount of time designated for each and whether they are urgent, important or can be postponed. Once you have a detailed layout of your upcoming day, all that is left for you is to follow it. One great tip is to leave some buffer time between each task so that, even when something urgent comes up, you still have an ample amount of time to get the others done.

Below are some great techniques that come recommended from some of the greatest minds to tackle the struggles with task prioritization.

Eat the Frog

As unrelated it seems, this is one of the most popular methods developed by Brian Tracy. The idea behind this approach to task prioritization is an interesting one. Brian thinks that if we were given a frog to eat at breakfast for the rest of our lives, nothing bad could ever top that. No matter how bad the rest of our day goes, once we have consumed the amphibian, we are done for the day. The frog, as you may have come to realize, refers to the most unwanted, boring and toughest task that one has on their to-do list. Brian suggests that it should be our goal to get it off the list first thing in the morning so that the rest of the day feels like a breeze. Here's how it can be applied in task management.

You have a set of tasks you need to perform. Start with placing them in four different categories which include the following.

- Category A: Tasks that you don't want to do but must do.
- Category B: Tasks that you don't want to do and can leave them as they are.
- Category C: Tasks that you want to do but don't have to.
- Category D: Tasks that you want to do and must do.

Once you have all the tasks organized like this, all that is left to do is start with the most uninteresting one, category A. The #1 reason why we keep avoiding something is that we find it too hard or boring.

However, imagine the relief you will experience once you are done with it and have the whole day to yourself to do whatever you feel like doing next. Once the hardest one is out of the way, the rest will seem like nothing but a piece of cake.

Eisenhower Matrix

This technique of prioritization was developed by Dwight D. Eisenhower and thus named after him. This consists of a four-quadrant visualization that helps individuals prioritize each task in the backlog. This doesn't require any preparation or tools but just a piece of paper and a list of tasks. According to Eisenhower, all tasks find their place in one of the four quadrants. The goal is to sort tasks based on their importance and urgency. Some tasks may be important but not urgent, some may be urgent but not important, some may be both urgent and important or neither.

The quadrants are as follows:

- High priority: Tasks that are both urgent and important.
- Medium Priority: Tasks that are important but not urgent, meaning they can be delayed. This quadrant is further divided into another quadrant with tasks that are urgent but not important.
- Low Priority: Tasks that are neither urgent nor important.

Using this method can help you create four separate lists and go forward with each, one after the other. The tasks that fall in the medium and low priority quadrants can be eliminated, postponed or delegated.

Ivy Lee Method

The Ivy Lee Method is more than a century old, yet is still used by some of the most successful brands and entrepreneurs worldwide. This comes in handy when we have more than what we can handle on our to-do lists. This allows its users to shortlist what tasks to attempt first and why.

Ivy Lee, the developer of the strategy, suggests that one must make a list of six of the most important tasks before going to bed for the following day. Based on their importance and urgency, prioritize them so that you can start with the most important and urgent one first thing in the morning. Only move onto the second task once you have accomplished the first one. Create another list for the following day before going to bed every night and make it a habit. This way, not only will you sleep better knowing what to work on exactly but also wake up feeling high-spirited and confident as you already have everything sorted out for the day.

Warren Buffet's Two-List Strategy

The worst thing that can happen is not knowing what goals to work on. You might have wanted to become an astronaut when you were young. However, now that you are in your mid-thirties and a management job, there is very little chance that you will become one. It is now more of a dream than an achievable goal. Sometimes, we keep focusing on the wrong goals which is why we need to keep reassessing our desires and wants from time to time. To do this, we need to evaluate our long-term goals so that we don't end up feeling regret. Warren Buffet, the most successful investor across the globe, presents his two-list strategy to help with this. He suggests dreamers list down twenty-five goals they want to achieve in life. These can be related to anything they are passionate about.

Once you have the list, shortlist five goals that you want to achieve at all costs from the twenty-five by circling them. What you are left with are twenty goals. What Warren suggests is that one must try to AVOID those goals at all costs. Had they been so important, they would have made the circled list but since they didn't, it means you don't think of them as too important. Meaning, even if you aren't able to fulfill them, you won't regret it. The same theory can be applied to daily tasks as well. Create a list and circle the most important ones. Then postpone, eliminate, or delegate the remaining ones.

ABCDE Method

Another one by Brian Tracy, the ABCDE method allows you to sort the many items from your checklist into a doable order. Start with a list of all the tasks you plan on attempting throughout the day, week or month. Next, sort them in any of these five categories mentioned below.

- A: Tasks placed in this section hold the most importance and have serious consequences if left undone. If there is more than one such task, you can label them as A1, A2, and A3... that way, A1 is your top priority.
- B: Tasks placed in this section are important but have minor consequences. For example, failing to accomplish these can make someone unhappy.
- C: Tasks in this section have no consequences. These are tasks that, if accomplished, would be nice but if left undone, won't create any problems for you or anyone else.
- D: Tasks placed in this section can easily be delegated and should be delegated. When you strategically delegate tasks, you free yourself up to focus more on the tasks in sections A and B.
- E: Tasks under this section must be eliminated as they offer no significant benefits to you or others. They are basically nothing but time wasters and can easily be omitted.

Scheduling and its Importance

Scheduling tasks ahead of time is another form of prioritization that involves having all the tasks planned and in writing. We do this in our daily or weekly planners, in to-do lists or calendar apps on our phones. We set reminders about tasks and important events which helps us stay ahead of our game and know exactly what is expected of us. To-do lists, in this respect, come in handy a lot. They are the quickest and most effective ways to have everything important jotted down.

The idea is to have everything in writing so that it doesn't escape the mind and gets done on time. This is what we mean with scheduling. This takes some burden off of our shoulders as we feel more prepared and thus, more productive. Scheduling also keeps our head clear and free from any sort of confusion. This allows us to stay more in control and deal with any unexpected outcomes or surprises easily. We also feel less exhausted with all the thinking that goes into determining what we should go for next as everything is laid out ahead of time.

However, sometimes, we are left with more than what we can handle and despite our best efforts, we fail to accomplish some. This doesn't look good in front of our superiors and can hurt our reputation. Therefore, before we end this chapter, how about we take a brief look to help you get started with scheduling. Think of it as the basics on how to get started with it, so that we can head on to learn the best means to manage time efficiently.

The Basics of Scheduling

Although there are countless apps to browse through, many free and user-friendly, there still is something about the pen and paper method that wins for many. It just leaves the list creator with some sense of pride as they jot down everything in great detail so that they don't have to waste time later. The satisfaction is quite incomparable to typing into an app. If this is the first time you are creating a to-do list, then here's all the information you need to get started.

Spot Free Time

Many individuals struggle with assessing how much time they have in the day. Some don't even consider the value of calculating the working hours. But it is crucial, as even when we say we work a 9 to 5 shift, we aren't technically spending every minute of it working. If we don't account for the time we actually invest in working, we will never be able to identify how to schedule tasks. This is one reason why many of us pile on more than we can handle in a day and feel guilty when we aren't able to fulfill all of them. Therefore, start with knowing the exact amount of available work hours so that you don't overschedule.

Schedule Your Actions

Next comes the job of scheduling all those actions that will eventually lead to the completion of a task. This involves gathering all the required tools, having everything researched prior and eliminating distractions. These mentally prepare you to begin and help you maintain focus to give your best shot at anything.

Plan Priority Tasks

Of course, next, the goal should be task prioritization. Go through the list of all the tasks and see what tasks must be done first and what can be delayed. Next, spot all such tasks that only you can accomplish and delegate the rest. When scheduling tasks, schedule the most important ones during the time of the day you are most productive. That way you will be able to put in your best work as you feel more focused and keen.

Schedule Breaks in Between

It is great if you are someone that moves from one task to another one right away, but let's face it: it isn't realistic. You have to allow your mind to relax and rejuvenate. This is why no to-do list will be complete without short breaks in between. They are also beneficial when something urgent comes up and you have to do it first. Once it is completed and you are still keen on completing the remaining tasks, you can cut short some time from each break session and spend it doing the remaining tasks.

Task Scheduling Tools

When it comes time to get scheduling, we have the following tools at our disposal.

Daily or weekly planners: Daily planners help employees become more organized. They are a great way to schedule the biggest as well as the smallest tasks. You can use a notebook to jot things down or turn to some professional planner app to put in everything. You can even set timers and reminders/alarms once the time for each task is up. Another benefit is increased productivity as everything you need is already planned. So, you won't have to lose focus or momentum going back and forth, worrying about what to do next.

Calendars: Everyone thought that once planners took over calendars would become outdated, but boy were they wrong. There are still so many staunch calendar schedulers who believe that having a wide and visible view of what you are supposed to be doing is the best way to stay focused. Calendars are especially handy when there is more than one person scheduling things. For instance, it can be great for a department or team and serve as a notice board with all the upcoming events and deadlines put in. Like planners, they aim to also make your life easier and that is exactly what they do. Finally, they are great for people who still haven't converted to complete digitalization and want to remain devoted to the good old methods of getting things done.

Daily Action Plans: Daily action plans consist of all the tasks one plans to take on during the day. They only differ from planners and calendars in the way they are created. They are a more elaborative take on a planner as they not only list down all the tasks to be performed but also the means, resources, and steps to accomplish them. Their elaborateness is what makes them so popular. You not only know what you need to do but also know what tools you will require and what steps will you take to get those tasks off the list.

Chapter 7:

Techniques That Improve Time

Management

Hard work can be extremely draining and exhausting. This is why the new approach to managing work doesn't suggest working harder any longer. It was when the industrial revolution happened that employees were asked to work harder. However, working harder or working longer hours didn't drastically improve productivity. What did, was working smarter. The concept of working smarter and not harder suggests that one eliminates all those menial and repetitive tasks that waste time and only focus on the ones that reap the most benefits and make a difference. It is considered to be one of the most brilliant techniques for working which doesn't leave the worker all sweaty and mentally-saturated. In this chapter, before we head on to listing the best ways to manage available time, we must understand why our focus should be on working smarter and not harder.

Working Hard is Physically Exhausting

Working hard drains our energy reserves. It leaves us with very little mental and physical strength to work on more meaningful and important things in life like our family and relationships. Therefore, if you wish to avoid such mental exhaustion that makes you groggy and drained of energy, save your time by delegating and automating repetitive tasks. Identify areas where some minor changes in the work processes can improve productivity and save time. Delegate tasks whenever necessary and perform similar tasks simultaneously. You will also feel happier and less stressed.

Working Hard Wastes Time

...Or to put it more aptly, working smart saves time. When you work smarter, you conserve energy and ultimately, save time. You feel more in control which works as a booster for your productivity. However, it isn't as simple as that. Working smarter also involves giving your best, even when it takes you hours to get something done. But keep in mind that no one can work for hours straight. Breaks and little pauses in between are a must. When you save time, you will have more time left to work on other tasks and do something creative rather than just slop it together.

Working Smarter Enhances Productivity

That is a given, now isn't it? Working hard does have its perks but not as many as working smart does. The biggest, of course, is increased productivity. But haven't we already repeated that several times? The reason stressing it over and over is important is because it streamlines processes and reduces the costs. Not to mention, it also saves labor. Aim to combine similar tasks and try to minimize the steps needed to conduct a task. The fewer steps there are, the less time it will take you and the more efficient and productive you will be in doing them.

Working Smarter Adds Value

Ask any manager, and chances are their ideal candidate as an employee would be someone who knows how to get most done using limited resources. If you are that person, your chances for landing your ideal job at a pay rate you dream of increase exponentially. Working smarter is no less than a skill that helps individuals stand out from the crowd. As an employer, when you hire the best people for your business, your costs reduce and your productivity improves. You feel more confident and become a well-reputed name in the industry.

Spilling the Beans with 25+ Time Management Tips and Hacks

As stated throughout the book, the key to effective time management in our professional and personal life lies in how we value and spend our time. We are all given the same amount of hours in the day, yet many can get more done. How they do that is what we need to learn as well because, at the end of the day, it is how we feel and see ourselves. Do we see ourselves as a winner, successful, or a failure, a letdown?

The surprising thing to note here is that it doesn't come down to how much time we spend working. It comes down to how we spend it and doing what. Imagine this: you work all day and barely get all the tasks on your list scraped off. And then there is your coworker who can rarely be seen at his desk all day but is still the brightest mind in the room. People come to him for advice, tips, and the managers just love him. He is always their priority when something urgent comes up. What makes him their favorite isn't just licking their manager's boots but how they can get everything done on time. They are reliable for a reason and that reason is nothing but excellent time management skills. They know what things are worth investing their time in, they know how much time each task deserves and finally, they know how to abstain from getting distracted once they get down to it.

You can be like that too and luckily, we can help you on your journey. Below are some of the greatest and most praise-worthy time management tips and strategies to implement to improve your effectiveness, performance, and efficiency.

1. Identify productivity patterns: Know what time of the day you work your best, are most focused and feel energized. This is the time when you are your most productive. Planning and doing the most important tasks of your day during those hours is the best way to get them out of your way. You will be able to accomplish things faster and experience increased satisfaction.

2. Develop a calling schedule: Set a time during the day to manage all your important calls. Leave the rest for after-work hours. Those aren't important. If they were, they would have made your schedule or to-do list. Allow them to go to voicemail and respond to them afterwards. The best time to manage calls is during lull periods.

3. Focus your energy on things you can control: There is no point wasting your time, resources, or energy over things that aren't in your control. Focus on the ones you can control. The time you spend worrying or staying anxious is time wasted. You could have easily done other things rather than worry about everything.

4. Create a Consistent Routine: Routines help you streamline things in your life. They help you stay organized and focused. When you follow a consistent routine every day, it becomes a part of you. It becomes who you are and you start doing them automatically, even when no one is watching. Therefore, aim to create routines that are in line with your goals and plans.

5. Stay Positive: When you feel negative, everything around you becomes negative as well. When you focus on the negative aspects of things more, you take in the same vibes. Your productivity suffers, too. Maintaining a positive attitude towards things is pivotal for your success.

6. Stay healthy: Eat healthy and stay healthy. Give your body and mind the relaxation it needs. This has a direct effect on your energy. Enjoy a proper night's rest. When you feel low and enervated, there is very little chance that you will perform your best. So focus on eating the right things, exercise so your body doesn't give up on you, and practice mindfulness so that your brain gets an escape from the chaos.

7. Develop an action plan: Actions plans work wonders to help you accomplish tasks you schedule daily. An action plan serves as a lighthouse shedding light on things. Having a course of action helps you stay focused and not give in to the many

temptations. A well-devised action plan lists all the steps you need to perform the task, has details about the required resources, and has a time limit dedicated for each task so that you don't fall prey to distractions.

8. Focus on long-term goals: You may not be getting everything right lately and think about giving up. But it is only because you are so focused on your present goals that you have lost sight of the long-term ones. They are the ones you should be focused on. Forget postponing plans for the future. Start working on them today and take out the time for them at some point during the day or weekend. They are the ones that will lead you to success, not the unimportant ones you are so keen on taking up and accomplishing.

9. Have a to-do list to begin with: Similar to action plans, to-do lists also work the same way. They fulfill the same purpose as any action plan. The only difference is that they only offer an overview of the things you need to do, not how to do them. However, you can go as extensive as you want to and add time frames, steps, and repercussions. You can even have more than one for each different task and plan ahead. Making one will definitely reduce stress.

10. Make decisions when they are due: Putting off important decisions for a later date isn't the best habit to have. But that doesn't mean you have to be hasty. Evaluate the pros and cons of every day and if you think you have all the information you need, then there is no point delaying it. However, if you are certain that if you wait something good will come, then wait.

11. Start your day early: Take notes from the lives of Ernest Hemmingway, Tim Cook, and Thomas Jefferson, as they all were early risers. They called it the most productive time of the day as there are little to no distractions during the wee hours. You can go through the details of how you are going to tackle the day so that when you head to the office, you know exactly where to start from. If that isn't the best tip of all, we don't know what is.

12. Set Rewards for yourself: Rewards are the best way to find that lost motivation that you need to get through the day. Setting rewards also prevents you from procrastinating. The best tip is to set rewards that genuinely tempt you. That way, you will try to get done with things as fast as you can so that you can enjoy the fruits of your effort. Motivation and drive is what increases productivity.

13. Automate repetitive tasks: The best way to make the most of your time is by automating tasks that are repetitive in nature. Spot these early and then try to avoid them at best. Repetitive tasks are those tasks that you have to do every single day. However, if there is the slightest chance that they can be delegated or eliminated altogether, make that happen. An example of this can be typing emails or sending out letters. If most of them look similar (start or end on the same note), create a template for everyday use and use it to minimize the time spent on writing individual ones.

14. Attempt things that require discipline first: When you learn to commit to taking on the hardest things first thing in the morning, it sets a positive tone for the rest of the day. Another reason to do them first is because they require the most effort and to put that in, you need to be energized and focused. When is that time? You guessed it right –mornings. When you challenge yourself and ace at it with consistency and improved focus, you are bound to feel great the rest of the day. The remaining tasks will feel easy, too.

15. Run errands in one go: If you need resources and tools to get started on something, have them gathered in one attempt. Going back and forth for things breaks tempo and thus, affects productivity. If your goal is to improve your efficiency, then this is the best way to do so. This will also save you time.

16. Keep a calendar: When you have everything marked in a calendar, there are fewer chances of you forgetting anything. This is ideal for those who have to make appearances a lot and struggle with dates. Having a calendar on your phone or in your

room like old times is a great way to reduce the chances of forgetting deadlines and important business events.

17. Reassess practices: Since everything keeps evolving so rapidly, the best way to reduce the amount of time wasted over menial things is to embrace technology and evolve your way of doing things. New technology keeps changing the processes and if you are persistent with using the old outdated ones, then you are the only one at loss here. Keep researching for the best practices and processes so that you can stay ahead of everyone and be done with everything in less time.

18. Keep an idea diary: An idea can strike at any time. Something great and innovative may come to you when you are brushing your teeth, driving to work or taking a shower. However, not noting them down the moment they strike can be detrimental. Thus, keep a pocket diary on you at all times so that nothing great leaves your mind without being recorded. You can always go back and review them during your free time and see if they are worth the effort or not. The ideas can be task-related as well.

19. Be proactive: Being proactive means managing any issues and problems the moment they arise. Putting them off for later will leave them to fester and grow which means additional complications in the future.

20. Know when to say no: Overcommitting yourself to things that weren't even yours to do isn't smart at all. The best way to gain respect from others is by proving your worth through your work. However, if you keep missing deadlines and remain engaged in someone else's work, poor reputation will be the last thing you will have to worry about. Therefore, know your limitations and prioritize your work first. Only commit to other things when you have the time.

21. Know your limits. Don't waste time on unproductive tasks. When something comes up that is out of your area of

knowledge or expertise, find some help or an alternative way to get it done.

22. Stop obsessing over perfectionism: it is a good idea to revise things when better ideas come along, but there is a fine line between that and obsessing over perfectionism. Keep realistic expectations because you will be the only person disappointed the most when you fail to fulfill them. Know when it is time to move on to something else.

23. Value down time: Down time is the time spent on things like traffic, waiting lines or during your commute. It is the time you must spend doing nothing productive. However, you can make the most of it by spending it resourcefully. You can listen to recordings, podcasts, market trend news, or make personal but important phone calls.

24. Track how much time each project takes: Since we are talking about time management, it would be remiss of us not to suggest time-tracking. Time-tracking is essential because it tells you if your current state needs improvement or not. Time-tracking gives you a baseline to measure your progress. It also helps with predicting how long each task will take so that you can schedule better.

25. Explore shortcuts: There may be other means to reaching an end in less time and with little resources, you just need to discover it. Exploring your options is a great way to reduce the time spent on a task. See if there is some other way to do the task more efficiently and if there is, pursue that course of action.

26. Have a not to-do list: A not to-do list is a list that has all those tasks that you mustn't waste your time doing. These are usually the things that you will regret wasting time on later or abandon them halfway.

27. Know when to put the phone down: Economize your conversations by cutting them short. Know when to end one

and get back to doing your work. Unnecessary conversations, be it on the phone or face-to-face, waste valuable time. Thus, be mindful of how much time you spend attending to them.

28. Declutter your space: Organizing your workstation is another great productivity tip as it allows you to stay focused on the tasks at hand. A de-cluttered space is efficient. All the things you need are placed in an orderly manner, which subconsciously prepares you to start working right away.

Chapter 8:

30 Days Productivity Challenge

1	2	3	4	5
Wake up an hour early	Create To-do lists	Use the Eat the Frog Method to finish MITs first	Set your phone aside during working hours	Don't browse the Internet aimlessly
6	**7**	**8**	**9**	**10**
Write a summary of your day	Make time to set up a calendar	Learn to say no	Write down your goals and priorities	Organize your workstation
11	**12**	**13**	**14**	**15**
Sort out your inbox	Plan the next day before bedtime	Reward yourself with some free time	Divide big tasks into smaller ones	Take a rest because you deserve it

16	17	18	19	20
Work on Time Wasters	Forgo procrastinating	Create deadlines for all your tasks	Schedule breaks in between tasks	Download efficiency-improving apps
21	22	23	24	25
Finish an overdue task	Sleep for good 8 hours	Turn off the TV	Review your processes and see if they can be improved	Reduce water-cooler talks
26	27	28	29	30
Reward yourself	Limit call times	Invest in planners	Keep track of time by tracking it	Meditate and exercise

Conclusion

Time will always be a scarce resource. Not making the most of your day will only make you dread it later. In this book, we have dealt with some of the most common and recurring problems people face with time management. They complain of not having enough time or energy to go after the things they want to go after. But here's the thing: you that will have to change. Time waits for no one and will remain a constant. How you make the most of it is an art that we aimed to teach. The only way you will achieve success in your life is if you value time like it should be and utilize it wisely. Ideally, you should spend it doing the things that really matter so that when you look back, you don't regret running after things you later abandoned in life.

Hopefully, the ideas shared in this book will help you manage time in an efficient and effective way. But before we say our goodbyes, how about doing a quick recap of all the things that have been discussed in the book to refresh your memory? Let's see how many of these can you recall.

In the first chapter, we talked about what time management is and took a little history tour to when we started to track time. Then we moved on to discussing the uncountable benefits of managing time and later determined if you were a time waster or not.

In the second chapter, we dealt with some of the most common and avoidable time wasters and learned if we can resist temptations or not.

Following that, we talked about the biggest problem of all–procrastination. We talked about what it was, why we do it and how we can overcome it to become more productive. Then, with the help of many ideal research studies, surveys and experiments, we explored the connection between time management, productivity, and ultimately success. The following chapters discussed in great depth the different time management styles, the daily routines of many successful men and women, scheduling and prioritizing the need to improve skills and finally, the 25+ strategies to manage time more efficiently. Sounds like a lot to take in, right? However, if you stuck around until the end, it means you are ready to change your life for the better. You now have all the tools you need to pave your way to success.

Remember, we are all rooting for you!

References

10 Ultimate Benefits of Time Management in the Workplace. (2018, November 3). Retrieved from https://www.liveandlearnconsultancy.co.uk/benefits-of-time-management/

Abella, A. (2018, May 1). 3 Time Management Myths That Are Making You Exhausted. Retrieved from https://www.calendar.com/blog/3-time-management-myths-that-are-making-you-exhausted/

Brown, E. G. (2015, April 14). The Hidden Costs Of Interruptions At Work. Retrieved from Fast Company: https://www.fastcompany.com/3044667/the-hidden-costs-of-interruptions-at-work

Chun Chu, A. H., & Choi, J. N. (2010). Rethinking Procrastination: Positive Effects of "Active" Procrastination Behavior on Attitudes and Performance. The Journal of Social Psychology, 245-264.

Clement, J. (2019, August 14). Daily time spent on social networking by internet users worldwide from 2012 to 2018. Retrieved from Statista: https://www.statista.com/statistics/433871/daily-social-media-usage-worldwide/

Crutsinger, C. (1997). Thinking Smarter: Skills for Academic Success. Skylight Professional Development.

Hartz-Selley, D. S. (2014, March 11). Chronic stress is linked to the six leading causes of death. Retrieved from Miami Herald: https://www.miamiherald.com/living/article1961770.html

James-Enger, K. (2009, September 01). The pros of procrastination. Retrieved from Chicago Parent: https://www.chicagoparent.com/archives/pros-procrastination/

Kane, S. (2018, October 8). 10 Good and 10 Bad Things About Procrastination. Retrieved from https://psychcentral.com/lib/10-good-and-10-bad-things-about-procrastination/

Kashyap, S. (2019, June 24). Importance of Time Management in the Workplace. Retrieved from https://www.proofhub.com/articles/importance-of-time-management-in-the-workplace

Maddox, C. (2019, January 21). How to Minimize Employees Wasting Time At Work. Retrieved from Calendar: https://www.calendar.com/blog/minimize-employees-wasting-time-at-work/

Matei, A. (2019, August 21). Shock! Horror! Do you know how much time you spend on your phone? Retrieved from The Guardian: https://www.theguardian.com/lifeandstyle/2019/aug/21/cellphone-screen-time-average-habits

Miller, A. (2019, March 26). 6 Time Management Personalities and How They Manage Their Time. Retrieved from https://www.business2community.com/strategy/6-time-management-personalities-and-how-they-manage-their-time-02182249

Pozen, R. C., & Downey, K. (2019, March 28). What Makes Some People More Productive Than Others. Retrieved from Harvard Business Review: https://hbr.org/2019/03/what-makes-some-people-more-productive-than-others

Renzulli, K. A. (2019, April 11). An MIT study reveals 5 things highly productive people do every day—and you can start doing them today. Retrieved from https://www.cnbc.com/2019/04/11/mit-researcher-highly-productive-people-do-these-5-easy-things.html

Sanbonmatsu, D. M., Strayer, D. L., Medeiros-Ward, N., & Watson, J. M. (2013). Who Multi-Tasks and Why? Multi-Tasking Ability, Perceived Multi-Tasking Ability, Impulsivity, and Sensation Seeking. PloS ONE.

Smith, T. (n.d.). 130 Time Management Tips. Retrieved from http://www.littlethingsmatter.com/blog/2010/11/09/time-management-tips/

Solving Procrastination. (n.d.). Retrieved from https://solvingprocrastination.com/why-people-procrastinate/

Spencer, A., & Seaver, M. (2019, August 27). Want to Train Your Brain to Stop Procrastinating? Read These Tips From a Neuroscientist. Retrieved from https://www.realsimple.com/work-life/life-strategies/time-management/procrastination

Stringer, H. (2017). Boosting productivity. American Psychological Association, 54.

Text: Identify Your Time Management Style. (n.d.). Retrieved from https://courses.lumenlearning.com/waymaker-collegesuccess/chapter/text-identify-your-time-management-style/

The Shocking Truth about How Many Emails Are Sent. (2019, March). Retrieved from Campaign Monitor: https://www.campaignmonitor.com/blog/email-marketing/2019/05/shocking-truth-about-how-many-emails-sent/

Wang, W.-C., Kao, C.-H., Huan, T.-C., & Wu, C.-C. (2011). Free Time Management Contributes to Better Quality of Life: A Study of Undergraduate Students in Taiwan. Journal of Happiness, 561-573.

Wayne, J. S. (2014, February 20). 8 Reasons Why You Need To Work Smarter But Not Harder. Retrieved from https://www.lifehack.org/articles/productivity/8-reasons-why-you-need-work-smarter-but-not-harder.html